FORERUNNERS: IDEAS FIRST FROM THE UNIVERSITY OF
MINNESOTA PRESS

Original e-works to spark new scholarship

FORERUNNERS: IDEAS FIRST is a thought-in-process series of break-
through digital works. Written between fresh ideas and finished books,
Forerunners draws on scholarly work initiated ~~~ ~~~ le blogs, social
media, conference plenaries, jour~~~~ ~~~ ~~~ nergy of aca-
demic exchange. This ~~~ ~~~ ~~~ here intense
thinking, change, a~~~ ~~~ p.

la paperson
A Third University Is Possible

Akira Mizuta Lippit
Cinema without Reflection: Jacques Derrida's Echopoiesis and Narcissism Adrift

P. David Marshall
The Celebrity Persona Pandemic

Reinhold Martin
Mediators: Aesthetics, Politics, and the City

Shannon Mattern
Deep Mapping the Media City

Kelly Oliver
Carceral Humanitarianism: Logics of Refugee Detention

Davide Panagia
Ten Theses for an Aesthetics of Politics

Jussi Parikka
The Anthrobscene

Robert Rosenberger
Callous Objects: Designs against the Homeless

Chuck Rybak
UW Struggle: When a State Attacks Its University

Steven Shaviro
No Speed Limit: Three Essays on Accelerationism

Sharon Sliwinski
Mandela's Dark Years: A Political Theory of Dreaming

Callous Objects

Callous Objects
Designs against the Homeless

Robert Rosenberger

University of Minnesota Press

MINNEAPOLIS

Portions of this book were previously published in a different form in "Multistability and the Agency of Mundane Artifacts: From Speed Bumps to Subway Benches," *Human Studies* 37, no. 3 (2014): 369–92. Portions of chapter 6 were previously published in a different form in "On the Hermeneutics of Everyday Things: or, The Philosophy of Fire Hydrants," *AI & Society* 32, no. 2 (2017): 233–41.

Callous Objects: Designs against the Homeless by Robert Rosenberger is licensed under a Creative Commons Attribution-NonCommercial-NoDerivatives 4.0 International License.

Published by the University of Minnesota Press, 2017
111 Third Avenue South, Suite 290
Minneapolis, MN 55401-2520
http://www.upress.umn.edu

The University of Minnesota is an equal-opportunity educator and employer.

For Sabrina, from whom any good ideas I've had have been stolen

Contents

Introduction

WHY ARE BUS STOPS in particular a place where some homeless people prefer to sleep? Even if we've never been homeless ourselves, we can take a guess at what factors might be involved. Perhaps we've seen homeless people sleeping on benches in parks or subway stations, so we know that benches at bus stops—although designed for sitting—also afford homeless people a place to lie down. Surely another reason is the fact that bus stops are often equipped with a small rooftop and walls that offer some shelter from the rain, wind, and sun. If we are at all familiar with the dangers that come with sleeping on the street, then we might also guess that bus stops provide the relative safety of a well-trafficked and possibly well-lit public area.

But there is an additional factor that may be less obvious: bus stops afford a way to circumvent antiloitering laws that target the homeless. Cities often enact ordinances against sitting, lying down, sleeping, or simply spending too much time in public spaces. It can be argued that such laws are often designed specifically to force homeless people out of public areas. Thus the bus stop bench in particular not only offers a roofed and public place to lie down. It also offers plausible deniability: I was only waiting for the bus.

In this light, we see the shrewd political calculation of the vertical seat dividers, armrests, and handles that are so often added to bus stop benches. Such designs make it difficult or impossible to lie down across the bench. The design of such modified benches thus works together in conjunction with the antihomeless laws.

And yet it is possible to fail to notice all of this. This confluence of design and law can be so effective that everyday nonhomeless users of the bus stop may remain unaware of the location's status as a material and legal site of ongoing political dispute. With the homeless people themselves effectively scattered or prosecuted, with the law itself unnoticed, and with the design unobtrusive, the person who uses the bus stop each day simply as a space to wait for the bus may even remain largely unaware of the local problem of homelessness altogether.

The argument of this pamphlet is that law and design come together to force homeless people out of public space and into further danger and disadvantage. This treatment of the homeless, or the "unhoused" as some prefer, is immoral, unjust, and unnecessary. I join with homeless advocates who have long pressed this view and hope to draw out these issues in new ways through the use of ideas from social theory and the philosophy of technology.

This argument consists of two interrelated parts. The first is the task of exposing the empirical reality of the designs and laws that maintain a hold on our cities. We will need to take a look at the design of an assortment of everyday public-space devices, including garbage cans, ledges, fences, and signage. The bench will continue to serve as our guiding example. To make the moral argument, this pamphlet will not delve into the intricacies of ethical theory but will instead unearth, highlight, and test our moral intuitions. By raising awareness of the often unnoticed designs of our shared public space, and by reflecting on the often hidden political agendas behind them, I hope to demonstrate just how immoral and unjust these designs and agendas are.

This argument also involves the second task of considering the nature of technology itself. The philosopher Donna Haraway urges us to recognize technology's "noninnocence." Extending this line of thinking, we must develop a conception of technology's "guilt." We must think about what it could mean for a material "thing" to fall under political critique and even be criticized as callous. On one hand, of course, a device like a park or subway bench is simply an inert object, certainly not something with a mind or intentions, and thus obviously not among the category of things we would normally call "guilty" for any reason, let alone callous or cruel. But on the other hand, we must develop a way to understand objects like the bench as capable of participating in large-scale collective ends. It is crucial that we understand them to be things open to certain uses, closed to others, and amenable to concrete alteration by different social forces advancing different political objectives. Thus whatever form of callousness it is possible to attribute to technology, it will be a kind that is shared by a social collective. This accountability will be a distributed one, spread out across an assemblage of people and objects, all with real and specific consequences for people's lives. In what follows, I draw on insights from the philosophy and sociology of technology to develop an original account of the ways in which technologies are open to multiple meanings and uses and at the same time tailorable to specific agendas. There is a growing interest in what is sometimes called *hostile architecture,* and this elaboration of technological accountability in general, and this critique of antihomeless design in particular, adds to this line of thinking.

Applying these ideas to the topic of antihomeless design will again be a task of intuition management. An understanding of technological guilt will require challenging deep-seated cultural conceptions of technology as always either (or somehow both at the same time) inherently morally neutral or inherently part of forward thinking solutions. With this attempt to raise awareness of antihomeless law and design, combined with this exploration of the agency and even potential guilt of technology, we can put a spotlight on the callousness and injustice built into our everyday world.

1. Multistability

A BENCH is a straightforward example of a low-tech device. It is designed for the simple purpose of providing a place to sit. It accomplishes this by presenting a horizontal surface of appropriate size and height. The public-space bench, common to parks, train and subway platforms, and bus stops, is a suitable guiding example for our inquiry exactly because of its straightforwardness and simplicity.

As noted earlier, despite being designed, manufactured, and put in place for one purpose, benches are sometimes also used for

Figure 1. Subway bench with seat dividers, New York City, New York, USA. Photograph by the author.

1

a second. That is, although made for sitting, they are also sometimes used for sleeping, and this second option is at times taken
up by people living unhoused.[1] This second usage propels the bench
into the complicated legal and moral controversies over the issue of
homelessness, which spiral out into the politics of everything from
adequate housing, unemployment, and racial discrimination to domestic violence, addiction, and mental illness, among many other
thorny and important topics. And more, this second usage has in part
led to the enactment of controversial laws and has prompted strategic redesigns of public-space objects. Thus, despite its straightforwardness and simplicity, the bench is a moral and political flashpoint.

1. Homelessness can be defined in many ways. For example, if we look
at the 2015 "Annual Homeless Assessment Report" published by the U.S.
Department of Housing and Urban Development (HUD), we see a termi-
nological distinction made between those who do and do not make use of
shelter services. The term *unsheltered homeless people* is defined generally
as "people who stay in places not meant for human habitation, such as
streets, abandoned buildings, vehicles, or parks." *Sheltered homeless people*
are instead those who stay in "emergency shelters, transitional housing
programs, or safe havens." Distinctions are also made between those who
are temporarily homeless and those who are chronically homeless. The
chronically homeless can also be defined in many ways. This report defines
the *chronically homeless* as those "homeless individuals with disabilities
who have either been continuously homeless for a year or more or have
experienced at least four episodes of homelessness in the last three years."
See http://www.hudexchange.info/resources/documents/2015-AHAR-Part
-1.pdf. Some also use the term *homeless* to include those without their own
residence and who move from place to place, visiting friends and others
willing temporarily to put them up. For the purposes of this pamphlet, all
of the preceding definitions apply, and more. However, the focus here is on
those who spend significant parts of their lives in public spaces such that
they may be targeted by antihomeless laws and designs. While the primary
unhoused population under consideration here is thus the chronically
unsheltered homeless, the comments of this pamphlet apply as well to sheltered homeless people and others, because they too may spend significant
portions of daily life in public spaces. In addition, for some, the term *homeless* has become weighed down with negative connotations, and the term
unhoused is preferred. I use both here but mostly use unhoused and refer to
the issue itself as the problem of homelessness.

The philosophical challenge of accounting for a technology like the bench is to somehow develop a way to conceive of both its material specificity and its practical multiplicity. How should we think about an object that is at once designed for a specific purpose but is at the same time open to alternate uses and yet at the same time again still somehow remains limited in the ways it can possibly be used? Can we conceive of technology in a way that appreciates its concrete materiality and also its abstract ability to maintain different meaningful places in different people's lives?

To address these questions, we must first evaluate our intuitions about the nature of technology. To draw forward the potentially unreflexive and deeply held impressions about technology that might linger in the backs of our minds, let's consider some ideas from the philosophy of technology.

A central problem in the philosophy of technology, at least as I see it, is to figure out how to conceive of technology in a way that sees it as neither entirely determining our future nor entirely innocent of such determinations. Contemporary thinking on this point is haunted by two ghosts. One tradition of thought, sometimes called *determinist,* sees technology to carry us toward a certain future and to do so rather independently of our individual choices. "Utopian" determinists see technology as increasingly solving our problems. They look at the past, with its inferior medicine and food production and life-spans, and draw a line through the present and out into the future to predict a continuing positive vector of technological development. There are also "dystopian" determinists who see technology to be increasingly leading us to our doom. They perform the same basic maneuver as the utopians but come to the opposite conclusion. Their line from the past to the future runs through the increasingly destructive capacity of our weapons, environmental degradation, worker exploitation, or existential ennui. In contrast to both forms of determinism, there is an equally haunting tradition of thought, sometimes called *instrumentalist,* that sees technology as playing no role in shaping our lives whatsoever. In this view, technologies cannot ever be understood to be responsible in any way for anything. They are simply neutral and innocent instruments, subject entirely to our whims as users.

Contemporary thought in the philosophy of technology largely attempts to split the difference. Work in this field tries in many different ways to conceive of technology in a manner that is neither determinist nor instrumentalist. (The terms *instrumentalist* and, especially, *determinist* end up being used as insults flung at anyone who strays too far toward one of these positions.) That is, contemporary work attempts to tell a story in which neither *we* completely control technology nor *it* completely controls us. But versions of both determinist and instrumentalist thought certainly continue to shamble on throughout contemporary culture. They lurch undead in the backs of our minds in the form of unreflexive intuitions. As we work to conceive of the politics of public-space technologies, we must be careful not to stumble into either's grasp.

My favorite summary of this state of affairs is found in an interview with contemporary theorist Albert Borgmann.[2] He writes, "If there is one thing that the significant philosophers of technology agree on, it is this: Contemporary culture is pervasively technological, and technology is non neutral." This claim, itself astute, is also notable for what it implies: the significant philosophers of technology agree about, and only about, what technology is *not*. They agree that technology is not purely instrumental. The handy term *nonneutral* allows a person to be clear that she is not an instrumentalist without positively claiming to be a determinist. But although there is agreement over what technology isn't, there are still open questions about how we should understand what technology actually is.

My recommendation is that we think about technology through the notion of *multistability*. First developed by the philosopher Don Ihde, multistability refers to a technology's capacity to be taken up for different uses and to be meaningful in different ways. As Ihde puts it, "no technology is 'one thing,' nor is it incapable of belonging to multiple contexts."[3] Yet at the same time, a given device cannot simply be used for just any purpose, nor can it be meaningful in simply any way imaginable; the specifics of its concrete materiality—its particular physical composition—put limits on which uses and meanings are possible. In this terminology, only some relationships between a user and a technology prove to be "stable" within the experience of users. That is, a user's relationship with a technology is open to multiple "stabilities."

The notion of multistability comes to us through a tradition of philosophy called *phenomenology*. Phenomenology approaches philosophical problems from the entry point of the deep description of human experience as it is lived. That is, rather than start with a science-style God's-eye view on human beings, phenomenology begins by describing experience itself, putting on hold our received wisdom and concepts as much as possible, even ideas as basic as "subjects" and "objects."[4]

Ihde develops a phenomenological account of technology. He explains that technologies should not simply be counted among all the objects in the world that we experience, as if they are merely another thing that we perceive or act upon. Technologies play a "mediating" role in experience. They come between the user and the world, transforming the user's abilities to perceive and act. In this way, the technological mediation of user experience is nonneutral. Peter-Paul Verbeek, also working in this line of thinking, goes so far as to claim that it is through technological mediation that the user and the world become who they are. As he puts it,

3. Ihde 1999, 47; see also Whyte 2015.

4. In particular, Ihde is the grandfather of a contemporary school of thought called "postphenomenology," which combines insights from the philosophical traditions of phenomenology and American pragmatism and applies them to issues of technology usage. This pamphlet is a work of postphenomenology. See, e.g., Ihde 2009; Hasse 2015; Rosenberger and Verbeek 2015.

"when a technological artifact is used, it facilitates people's involvement with reality, and in doing so it coshapes how humans can be present in their world and their world for them."[5]

The notion of multistability thus points out that a technology always has the potential to mediate human experience in multiple ways. There is always more than only one possible path for a given technology to transform a user's ability to act on, perceive, and understand the world. And simultaneously, the materiality of that technology places limits on what those potential acts, perceptions, and understandings may be. This understanding of materiality is in tune with the work of Susan Bordo when she writes that "'materiality,' in the broadest terms, signifies for me finitude. It refers to our inescapable physical locatedness in time and space, in history and culture, both of which not only shape us (the social constructionist premise, which I share with the postmodernists) but also limit us (which some postmodernists appear to me to deny)."[6]

With all this said, it will still most often be the case that there is a main purpose to which a technology is put, a chief manner in which that technology tends to be taken up by most users. Again following Ihde, we can refer to this most common usage as "dominant." That is, although a technology always remains usable through multiple stabilities, it will often retain a dominant stability. And most often, this dominant stability will be the purpose for which the device has been designed and manufactured.

Let's use a simple example to show how these concepts work: Ihde's attempt to brainstorm different possible uses for a hammer. He writes, "A hammer is 'designed' to do certain things—drive nails into a shoemaker's shoe, or into shingles on my shed, or to nail down a floor—but the design cannot prevent the hammer from (a) becoming an objet d'art, (b) a murder weapon, (c) a paperweight, etc."[7] The hammer is thus multistable, and its dominant stability

5. Verbeek 2011, 7.
6. Bordo 1997, 181–82.
7. Ihde 1999, 46.

is the purpose of hammering, set in its usual context of building and fixing, workbenches and nails. The hammer was made for this dominant stability; that is, this is the function for which the hammer has been designed, created, distributed, and sold. As a form of technological mediation, when a person uses the hammer through this dominant stability, it transforms his ability to bang nails into something. But alternative stabilities are available too. The hammer can be used to hit and hurt someone else, an act that, I can only presume, would require a different kind of swing. Rather than finding its place on the workbench, the hammer can sit on a desktop and hold a stack of papers in place. It can find new meaning as a piece of found art. Surely further stabilities are possible, and surely many exist in actual practice. At the same time, owing to the specific materiality of the hammer, limited as it is to being only some sort of handle with a hammer head, this device cannot be used to do simply anything or to mean simply anything.

Think again of our guiding example of the bench. The public-space bench, just like any technology, is multistable. The dominant stability is that purpose for which it was designed, manufactured, purchased, and installed in a public area: it provides a place to sit. The public-space bench mediates user experience, transforming this point of the world into a location that affords sitting. Of course, it is possible to think of alternative stabilities. Cyclists sometimes use benches as makeshift bike racks. Joggers sometimes lean against benches to do stretches. With what I swear has always been the utmost cleanliness, and with the help of a diaper bag and changing pad, I have used benches on occasion as a changing table.

But of course the alternate stability of the public-space bench at issue here is its potential use as a bed, and in particular its pervasive use for just this purpose by unhoused people. For those without shelter, a bench of a standard design is something that affords sleep. It does so not only because of the contingencies of its material design but also because of its location in public space. For example, if the bench is in an area trafficked by other members of the community, and is thus in the view of many people, then it can sometimes offer a level of safety not found otherwise alone in the city's margins.

And the bench is in many ways a microcosm for the dynamics of public space itself. Following this conception of the bench, with its dominant stability, and its alternate stability sometimes taken up by people living unhoused, we can think about the multistability of public space generally.

We can consider the dominant purposes and meanings of public space. That is, we can think about the various features of public space and consider their interlocking dominant stabilities. The streets enable local transit. They provide a means for businesses to transport their goods and for people to travel by car and by other modes. Sidewalks enable foot traffic. Bus stops, as well as train and subway platforms, provide areas for travelers to wait for public transportation. Urban plazas offer meeting places and areas to sit outside for lunch. Public parks provide the community with shared spaces for outdoor recreation, relaxation, exercise, and gathering. They serve as event spaces. They provide vital green space. Their playgrounds provide areas for children to spend time. Their trees provide shade. Their presence can increase property values. By providing beneficial outdoor amenities for the community, they serve local business interests. These are just a few of the interconnected dominant uses of public space.

Against this broad sketch of the general dominant stability of public space stands an alternative in which unhoused people find a place to live. The streets and sidewalks become not only travel routes but areas in which to spend time. Garbage cans are not only waste receptacles but also a source of recyclables that can be collected and traded in for a modest income. Garbage cans may also be sources of food. Underpasses provide a form of shelter. Railways become walkable arteries. Shopping carts provide a means for moving and storing personal items. Empty coffee cups are used for panhandling. Alleyways, hillsides, roadsides, and other in-between areas—those interstices of city space—provide places to camp. Public parks become living spaces. For some, the city itself is home.

Thus we see in the standard configuration of public space both a dominant stability and a well-developed alternative stability. We see a dominant stability, to put it even more generally, that involves zones used for transit and recreation, with objects and layouts arrayed in tune with the purposes for which they were originally made and installed, and all this happening in accord with prevailing community and business interests. We also see an alternative stability in which those living unhoused, out of necessity, take up those same zones as a form of habitation. For those who have no experience with homelessness, this at times highly visible alternative usage of our shared space can serve as a reminder of the plight faced by the unhoused. It can serve as a reminder as well that the public interest does not reduce to business interest.

But the story does not end here. This is just the start of an account of both the multistability of technology in general and public space and its implications for homelessness in particular. Even though the standard designs and layouts of public spaces leave them open to these alternative usages by unhoused people, we will see efforts in design and law that target and restrict these stabilities. To account for these forces, we must turn next to social theory.

2. Sociality

IT IS NOT UNCOMMON to find public-space benches fitted with design features that discourage or prohibit their use as beds. Popular options include vertical partitions that separate each sitting space and armrests that similarly divide up the bench's surface. The websites of bench manufacturers rarely advertise the fact that these designs are specifically intended to discourage sleeping, although on occasion such partitions and armrests are referred to as "antiloitering" features. And of course, a wide variety of other design options, from curved surfaces to bucket seating, can perform

Figure 2. Park bench with armrest and seat incline, Tokyo, Japan. Photograph by the author.

this same antisleep function. The picture of the New York City subway bench included in the previous section is a prime example of an antisleep design.[1]

Public-space bench designs can be made to play into any number of social agendas in addition to deterring the presence of the unhoused. For instance, take the bench in Tokyo's Ueno Park shown in Figure 2. In an influential piece on antihomeless design in Japan, Yumiko Hayakawa claims that, in addition to featuring antisleep armrests, the slight slant of the seat of this bench is also designed to be slightly uncomfortable.[2] The goal is to discourage sitting too long and to encourage traffic flow through the park. Hayakawa reports that Ueno Park, the oldest public park in the entire country, is known to be a destination for unhoused sleepers. The bench designs in the park (and, in my observation, considering the park's size, their striking overall scarcity) reflect the city's effort to discourage the unhoused from taking up too much visible public space.

To capture these dynamics in which social forces intervene on the design of a technology to forward an agenda, we must turn to social theory.

Some of the most innovative and influential thinking on the philosophy of technology over the past three decades has been conducted in the field of science and technology studies (STS). Using sociological and anthropological methodologies, STS researchers investigate the ways that technologies are shaped by the rivalries that occur between social groups. As Nelly Oudshoorn and Trevor Pinch put it, "technological development emerges as a culturally contested zone where users, patient advocacy groups, consumer organizations, designers, producers, salespeople, policy makers, and intermediary groups create,

1. In his influential book *City of Quartz,* Mike Davis (1990, 233) refers to these designs as "bumproof benches." Here I use the less elegant term *antisleep benches.* See Rosenberger 2014b.

2. Hayakawa 2006.

negotiate, and give differing and sometimes conflicting forms, meanings, and uses to technologies."[3]

Because these theories conceive of technologies as potentially adoptable by different social collectives, we can interpret them here to be roughly amenable to the phenomenological notion of multistability. It is my contention that by combining our account of multistability with the insights of STS theories of technology, we can develop an innovative and helpful scheme for articulating how social forces can come to close off or open up a technology's various stabilities. This in turn will enable us to chart out the various social strategies involved in the design and experience of antihomeless technologies.

The particular STS account that I would like to consider here is Bruno Latour's *actor-network theory* and specifically the way it pertains to everyday technologies or, as he calls them, "mundane artifacts."[4] Under Latour's view, when we account for the ways a group comes together to enact an agenda, we should consider not only the people who belong to that group but also the technologies that they enlist. The group, or "network" as it is called in this vocabulary, is made up of a variety of "actors," and these actors can be either humans or "nonhumans," such as technologies. Actor-network theory thus gives a social account of technology, one that understands what a device does in terms of its role in a social collective.

In this view, technologies are not neutral or innocent objects. They are active players within ongoing rivalries between networks. A network's agenda, or "program of action," as Latour calls it, is not reducible to the agency of some individual actor but emerges from the collective agency of the overall network. Under this view, a technology that has been enrolled into a network now becomes an active contributor to the network's overall

3. Oudshoorn and Pinch 2003, 24.
4. Latour 1992.

aims. But that same object could always be wrestled loose and counter-enlisted into a rival network.

To understand a technology's role within a network, Latour provides a simple formula: "every time you want to know what a nonhuman does, simply imagine what other humans or other nonhumans would have to do were this nonhuman not present."[5] We can conceive of a technology as adopting some of the competencies of the people whose work that device has been brought on board to perform. When we enlist a technology into a network to perform a particular job, we can be said to "delegate" that job to the device.

Latour clarifies these ideas with the description of another low-tech public-space device: the speed bump. From one point of view, a speed bump could be dismissed as a simple, neutral, inert lump in the ground. But from the perspective of actor-network theory, the speed bump is revealed to be the active site of a contestation between opposing networks. Imagine that you want to speed along a particular road. You could encounter a powerful network that wants you to slow down, one that includes the police department as well as the authority and resources of the state. This network has multiple options available. For instance, a police officer could be posted at the side of the road and assigned the task of issuing traffic citations to any drivers caught violating the speed limit. Or instead, in place of that officer, a speed bump can be built onto the road at that location, the task of the officer now delegated to this technology. (Latour notes that in some countries, a speed bump is referred to as a "sleeping police officer.") In both cases, the speeding driver is compelled to comply. Otherwise, she faces either a speeding ticket or a damaged suspension.

To articulate these social and material dynamics, Latour borrows from Madeleine Akrich's *script theory*. Under this account, as members of a collective play their parts in larger group agen-

5. Ibid., 229.

das, they can be understood to follow social scripts. This is true not only for human actors but for technologies as well. As Akrich puts it, "like a film script, technical objects define a framework of action together with the actors and the space in which they are supposed to act."[6] Following Akrich, we can use the term *material inscriptions* to refer to the modifications made to a technology to enroll it into a network and make it better follow that network's social script. For example, in the case of the speed bump, we can imagine material inscriptions that could further embed this actor into the network and help it better perform its delegated task, such as adding striped paint to make it more visible to drivers or adding a sign at the side of the road to warn drivers of the bump.

The antisleep facets of public-space benches can be interpreted through the lens of this framework of concepts. Features of benches like armrests and seat partitions can be interpreted as material inscriptions. The larger social network that intends to discourage the unhoused from using public-space benches as beds inscribes this program of action into these devices themselves. The antisleep benches are thus enrolled into this network and delegated the task of dissuading people from sleeping in public in this manner.[7]

Despite all that the actor-network account accomplishes with regard to describing the dynamics of the antisleep bench, my suggestion is that even more could be achieved through including a phenomenological conception of multistability. I have two reasons for this suggestion. First, a conception of the multistability of technology helps to account for why particular networks come into conflict over particular devices in the first place. The actor-network perspective understands the agency of a technology in

6. Akrich 1992, 208.
7. There are often calls for the development of an activist arm of the field of science and technology studies. Similarly within the field of philosophy in general, and within the philosophy of technology in particular, there are calls for engaged versions of philosophy. I intend for this pamphlet to serve as a contribution to exactly these moves toward engaged philosophy and activist science and technology studies.

Figure 3. Some examples of antisleep benches: sidewalk bench in Paris, France (upper left); bus stop in Philadelphia, Pennsylvania, USA (lower left); park bench in Salt Lake City, Utah, USA (upper right); wall-mounted bench in the London Underground, England (lower right). Photographs by the author.

terms of its role in a network. But this perspective appears to lack an account of a technology's readiness to participate in this or that particular action, and yet at the same time not just any action. The notion of multistability helps to fill this gap, and it does so because it is not an exclusively social concept but instead a philosophical conception of materiality. As a multistable material object, any technology is open to multiple uses and meanings and thus is open to enrollment in multiple networks.

The public-space bench is a case-in-point example. Actor-network theory is ideal for providing an account of the way the bench is altered as it is enrolled into one network and against another. But a notion of multistability is useful for accounting for what brought about this particular conflict over this device between these particular networks in the first place, namely, the bench's peculiar material readiness to be used as a bed and the contingent preexisting need of some unhoused people for this alternative stability.

The second reason that I recommend a combination of the notion of multistability with the insights of actor-network theory is that it enables us to develop a useful categorization of the ways that social forces interact with a technology's capacity to afford multiple uses.

Let's consider three ways that social agendas can relate to the multistability of technology:

1. *Restrictionary modifications*: A network can move to "close off" a technology's undesired stabilities. A multistable technology might offer more than one widely used stability, and a powerful social group may prefer to restrict the device in a way that renders it possible to use only through the group's own preferred stability. Through material inscriptions, the technology can be modified so that it is difficult or impossible to use in terms of the undesired stability. The central example of this chapter, in which benches are redesigned to make them difficult or impossible to use as beds, is a paradigmatic example of a restrictionary modification.

2. *Unrestrictionary modifications*: In a case in which a restrictionary move has been made, and a stability of a technology has been closed

off, a rival network may work to "reopen" that stability. Through its own counterinscriptive efforts, the rival network may attempt to lift those restrictions and reinstate the closed-off stability.

3. *Expansionary modifications*: Rather than closing off a stability, or reopening a formerly closed stability, it is possible to work to expand the ways that a technology could be used or to secure and enable multiple stabilities. Such modifications "open up" the possibilities for use.

This list is not exhaustive. For example, we could refine this breakdown further, even in its own terms. We could separate restrictionary modifications into at least two subcategories based on whether their restrictions come with more or less force. It is possible to distinguish between what could be called *prohibitory* modifications that attempt to make it impossible to utilize a device in terms of a particular stability and *dissuasionary* modifications that merely discourage that usage. We could consider a corresponding distinction that could be drawn within expansionary modifications. It may be possible at times to contrast *facilitationary* modifications that simply make a new stability available and what could be called *persuasionary* modifications that go further to actively encourage usage in terms of that new stability. Of course, there is a crucial context relativity to all of these categories. For example, what may be entirely prohibitory to one potential user may be merely dissuasionary to another user who possesses greater means to counter the work of that modification. It is surely possible to identify further refinements and even further classes of modification altogether. The point here is that the combination of a phenomenological conception of multistability with an actor-network account of material inscriptions makes this line of theorization possible.

In any case, in the analysis that follows, we will be guided mainly by the distinctions between restrictionary, unrestrictionary, and expansionary modifications. That is, we will focus on design strategies that close off, reopen, and open up the possible ways that users may take up their devices. These notions will help us address the various ways that multistable public-space technologies are subject to the tug-of-war of social and political forces. They will also help us to articulate the particular ways that antihomeless designs fit into larger political agendas—and how things could be otherwise.

Interlude: Spikes

In June 2014, a picture was posted to the social media website Twitter of a set of chrome spikes built into the ground in an alcove outside a London apartment building.[8] As noted in the tweet, the unmistakable intention behind this design feature was to prevent people from using the area as a place to sleep. The tweet went viral and was shared across the Internet, inciting outraged responses. Activists identified other instances of antihomeless spikes, including some elsewhere in London installed along a ledge outside a Tesco supermarket and some on the other side of the ocean outside a bookstore in downtown Montreal. An online petition was established that immediately accrued tens of thousands of signatures. Then mayor of London Boris Johnson joined in, tweeting, "Spikes outside Southwark housing development to deter rough sleeping are ugly, self defeating & stupid. Developer should remove them ASAP."[9] The mayor of Montreal similarly hopped aboard, tweeting, "The anti-homeless spikes are unacceptable!!!"[10] Protesters snapped pictures of themselves lying down beside the spikes. Others vandalized the spikes, covering them with concrete.

By the time the petition had cleared 130,000 signatures, the spikes were removed from the apartment building, the bookstore, and the supermarket.

Of course what makes the spikes a special case is their unhidden nature. They do not merely make it difficult or impossible to sit or sleep wherever they have been installed. They also communicate

8. Rosenberger 2014a.
9. Halliday and Siddique 2014.
10. QMI Agency 2014.

Figure 4. A wrought iron spike-studded strip set across a ledge in New York City, New York, USA (left), and a ledge set with chrome spikes in London, England (right). Photographs by the author.

in stark terms the message that unhoused people are not welcome. Those who take notice of antihomeless spikes are often struck by their similarity in design and strategy to those smaller versions mounted to signs and rooftops to shoo away pigeons. This ready comparison leads many to conclude that such spikes are inhumane, indeed almost identical to the treatment of pests.

Although the preceding story recounts a recent small victory in the struggle against antihomeless sentiment built into the urban environment, spikes and similar studs remain an utterly commonplace fixture of many urban spaces.[11] They can be found across any

11. Criminology researcher James Petty helpfully questions this narrative, suggesting that outrage over the London spikes does not indicate public support for the unhoused and instead reflects its overall discomfort with being reminded of the problem of homelessness altogether. See Petty 2016.

number of surfaces and ledges, sometimes built into the ground and sometimes under bridges and overpasses in the form of boulders, concrete pyramids, and cobblestone.[12]

My suggestion is that the case of antihomeless spikes presents us with a test of our moral intuitions. Because of their unmasked nature, and because of the visible outrage they have sparked, they present us with questions. We are prompted to ask ourselves if we share in the outrage over these actions against unhoused people. Does the use of spikes strike you as an immoral or unjust way for human beings to be treated? If so, then I suggest that this outrage commits you to similar moral discomfort with a variety of other antihomeless laws and designs. The spikes represent only the most brazen and least hidden edge of the larger and more pervasive effort in design and policy that targets the unhoused. The spikes are, so to speak, the pointy tip of the iceberg.

Whereas the spikes telegraph their intentions loudly and unmistakably, the antisleep bench is different. A design like the antisleep bench instead shuts down usage as a place to sleep while at the same time enabling usage as a place to sit, all without similarly broadcasting these dynamics. One could sit on the bench and remain unaware of its antisleep design. That is, one could easily spend time sitting on an antisleep bench without having any idea about its simultaneous role in denying unhoused people this particular site as a place to sleep and, generally, in contributing to a larger effort to flush the unhoused out of public space. Whether we consider the spikes, the benches, or the further designs and laws to be discussed in the following chapters, the effects are the same. The spikes are simply the most forthcoming about their intentions.

Thus, if your moral reasoning and intuition bring you to recognize that designs like the antihomeless spikes are no way to treat

12. One startling recent example was the new addition of spikes to alcoves along a New York City street just before a highly publicized visit by the pope. It appears that their intention was to clear away homeless people from the pontiff's potential sight lines. Carlson 2015.

fellow citizens and fellow human beings, then it turns out that you also hold an additional moral position: you should be additionally against the larger and less visible panoply of laws and designs that target the unhoused. And, incidentally, so should the mayors of London and Montreal.

Figure 5. Antipick recycle can with built-in lock, Denver, Colorado, USA. Photograph by the author.

3. Closing Off

GARBAGE CANS are another paradigmatic example of a multistable public-space technology. They sit at the intersection of a variety of competing social agendas. And despite what at first may appear to be a simple and innocuous construction, their designs reflect this fraught social status. For example, garbage cans in public spaces are often fit into cagelike outer structures made up of vertical metal slats. In addition to their standard usage as receptacles for trash, garbage cans have proven to afford graffiti writers a surface to mark with spray paint. The vertical slats disrupt this affordance by breaking apart the potential writing surface. (Manufacturers often market this design as a graffiti deterrent and also offer graffiti-resistant paint.)

There are also garbage cans built with clear exteriors. Such designs are sometimes an antiterrorism strategy. They make it easier to see the contents of the can and thus more difficult to hide a bomb.

The vertical slats and the clear exteriors are examples of "restrictionary" design modifications. Garbage cans have revealed themselves to be multistable in particular ways. These restrictionary redesigns work to "close off" particular stabilities. These particular garbage can exterior designs may be interpreted as material inscriptions that enlist the cans themselves into networks that aim to limit how they may be used.

Similar dynamics of garbage can design play out in terms of the problem of homelessness. Garbage cans are once again revealed to be multistable technologies in the way they sometimes serve several functions for people living unhoused. Some people use garbage cans as a source of recyclable materials. Such recyclables can often be exchanged for a small sum of money. Garbage cans are also sometimes approached as a source of discarded food.

Several redesign options are available to those who want to discourage these particular alternate usages of the garbage can. One common design strategy is the addition of a "rain hood." Such features do not merely prevent precipitation from entering the can or keep away animals; they also make it difficult for someone to reach down inside.

Another design feature of garbage cans that prevents trash picking is a locking mechanism. Often built into the case surrounding the can, or affixed to the outside, such locks limit who can access the contents inside. When combined with rain hoods or other designs that restrict access through the can's opening, locking mechanisms effectively prohibit picking. For example, the garbage can from Amsterdam featured in Figure 6 has a locking mechanism built into the frame. The one from New York City has a hasp and chain attached to the can's exterior, secured with a padlock. The recycle receptacles across downtown Denver, Colorado, consist of designs that prohibit picking (one of which is shown in Figure 5), and they feature a built-in locking mechanism.

These antipick garbage cans join with the antihomeless spikes and antisleep benches as examples of restrictionary designs aimed at the unhoused population. They all represent redesign strategies that close off a stability of a multistable technology. What I'm here calling "restrictionary" design is related generally to a growing trend of critique referred to variously as "hostile," "cruel," "disciplinary," "unpleasant," and "defensive" design and architecture.[1] Issues of hostile architecture are receiving increasing attention, and I hope to contribute to this trend with this critique of antihomeless design.

1. See, e.g., Savicic and Savic 2013; Lambert 2013; Quinn 2014; Chellew 2016. For collections of images of defensive architecture, see, e.g., the work of Dan Lockton, Nils Norman, and Cara Chellew at https://www.defensiveto.com/, http://architectures.danlockton.co.uk/architectures-of-control-in-the-built-environment/, http://www.dismalgarden.com/archives/defensive_architecture.

Figure 6. Some examples of antipick garbage cans: Buenos Aires, Argentina (top left); New York City, New York, USA (top right); New Orleans, Louisiana, USA (bottom left); Amsterdam, the Netherlands (bottom right). Photographs by the author.

The various restrictionary designs considered here are notable for the way they converge on the same user group, each tailored specifically to restrict stabilities that are taken up by people living unhoused. This brings us to a central piece of the argument of this pamphlet: an array of objects have been redesigned to push unhoused people out of public spaces. That is, I claim that a broad series of restrictionary redesigns of public-space technologies work together to close off stabilities that afford the unhoused a potential living space. We can see this in different ways and to varying degrees in different cities across the planet. A goal of these chapters is to identify, philosophically articulate, and critique these restrictionary design modifications.

Restrictionary design elements sometimes take on an auditory dimension. To deter certain groups from using particular spaces, some technologies alter the public soundscape. For example, on the less harmful end of the spectrum are storefronts that play a steady track of classical music or some other genre unpopular among youths to discourage them from loitering outside. A more insidious device used for the same purpose is the Mosquito noise projector, which emits an irritating, high-pitched sound that only the young can hear. The unhoused population is targeted with similar auditory strategies, such as when loud music or irritating noises are broadcast at night within parks to discourage their use as campsites.

The use of water is another simple strategy for deterring unhoused people from spending time in a particular outdoor area. If a bench or alcove is hosed off each night, the dampness may discourage visitors from sleeping there. Businesses and churches have been accused of installing nightly sprinkler systems for the exclusive purpose of warding off unhoused sleepers.[2]

Of course, a common design strategy for ensuring that unhoused people do not spend time in an area is simply to make

2. Examples of institutions accused of using sprinklers to deter unhoused sleepers include St. Mary's Cathedral in San Francisco and the Strand bookstore in New York City. See Fagen 2015; Goldensohn 2013.

it the case that nobody can spend time there at all. This is often achieved by putting up a fence, cage, or wall. It is not uncommon in urban settings to see fences standing tall around small green spaces, hillsides, or church steps. Cages are occasionally affixed atop heat exhaust grates. Dumpsters and other trash storage areas are often walled off. When cities delegate the task of addressing the problem of homelessness to a technology like a fence, this can involve a redistribution of responsibility across many actors in addition to the fence itself; it often effectively shuffles accountability from law enforcement to the parks department.

A large-scale and chillingly effective example can be found in the 1990s redesign of New York City's Pennsylvania Station. A massive railway terminal in Manhattan, Penn Station connects lines from Amtrak, New Jersey Transit, the Long Island Railroad, and the city's subway system. In his book *Sidewalk,* Mitchell Duneier conducts an ethnographic study of the lives of unhoused outdoor book sellers in the Greenwich Village area of the city, several of whom had spent much of their lives in Penn Station throughout the 1980s before being pushed out.[3] Duneier explains that as a sprawling interior complex of restaurants, stores, newsstands, and waiting areas, Penn Station afforded the unhoused a complete livable ecosystem. He writes, "To an unhoused person, the station offers all of the amenities for day-to-day survival."[4] Restaurants would often donate food. Abundant seating areas, alcoves, and the subway cars themselves provided places to sleep. Bathrooms provided places to wash (and more). There was an overabundance of tourists and travelers to panhandle. The building is climate controlled. And because the restaurants and stores are open to the public, one could spend time in the station without a train ticket.

All of this changed in the mid-1990s. Amtrak officials simultaneously set forth on strategic building redesigns and engaged in

3. Duneier 1999.
4. Ibid., 124.

a crackdown on behaviors like sleeping, using alcohol, panhandling, and trash picking. In a startlingly candid interview with an
Amtrak homeless outreach officer, Duneier learns that in addition
to ramping up the number and kind of citations that were issued
to unhoused people, much of the station was redesigned to cut off
many of their living practices. Ledges known to afford sleeping
spaces were reshaped. Renovations eliminated alcoves, enabling
law enforcement to more easily monitor every space. Other out-
of-sight areas were fenced off. The Amtrak officer explained, "We
used to see people sleeping on this brick ledge every night. I told
them I wanted a barrier that would prevent people from sleeping
on both sides of this ledge. This is an example of turning something around to get the desired effect."[5]

It is crucial to keep in mind that responsibility for the restrictionary design maneuvers under analysis should in no way be
understood to reduce to the original designers and engineers
themselves. Such responsibility is always distributed across networks of actors. A person or group of people is certainly responsible for drawing up, say, a particular antisleep bench's original
design specifications. But those individual designers are of course
responsible neither for that bench's mass manufacture nor for its
implementation in particular public spaces. That all requires the
work of a number of powerful actors.

This point is put into relief in cases of restrictionary designs in
which the designer himself did not purposefully design in those
restrictions. Such dynamics are at work in one of my favorite
bench designs, the single-seater wall-mounted benches of Laurier
Station in Montreal, Canada. This bench features five individual
ovals each attached to the wall, two of them lower than the other
three. Strikingly, a ghostly afterimage of the previous metro riders floats above each seat, their shapes stained over time into the
station's granite walls as the procession of passengers' heads has

5. Ibid., 132.

Figure 7. Wall-mounted subway seating, Montreal, Canada. Photograph by the author.

slowly marred the surface like salad dressing on a countertop. The Laurier bench is functionally an example of an antisleep design. One effect of the differing heights of the individual bench seats is to prohibit one from lying across them.

However, the designer of Laurier Station, Jean-Paul Pothier, had intended the low seats to be used by children.[6] It is laudable when designs such as Pothier's take care to address the needs of multiple user groups. And in the case of the Laurier Station bench, we see an instance in which implementation and usage do not reduce to designer intent. The Laurier bench's antisleep effect appears to exist independently from the designer's intentions. But the antisleep function of this bench fits into a larger trend at work in Laurier Station in which benches follow the Pothier single-seater design, or hand-rail-style wall-mounted leaning bars for the disabled. As a ride through the Montreal Metro attests, the benches of other stations without antisleep features are often used by sleepers.

An additional important trend to note in restrictionary anti-homeless design is the move to eliminate devices altogether. For example, it may be decided that, rather than risk affording a place to rest, a ledge should be removed entirely. It is not uncommon for cities to eliminate or relocate benches to deter unhoused sleepers. Suburban neighborhoods sometimes enter fierce debates over whether they should have sidewalks, because their absence could discourage unwanted visitors to the area from walking through.[7]

This sort of strategy can help to explain the sometimes baffling experience of spending time in a public space that has been built without expected amenities. A park may be suspiciously devoid of sitting areas. Roadsides may lack expected sidewalks. Public drinking fountains may be entirely absent. Sidewalks in hot regions may continue along without trees or other forms of shade.

6. http://www.stm.info/en/info/networks/metro/laurier.
7. See, e.g., Reinan 2014; Lazo 2013.

According to Mike Davis in his bleak history of Los Angeles, California, *City of Quartz,* "public toilets, however, are the real Eastern Front of the Downtown war on the poor. Los Angeles, as a matter of deliberate policy, has fewer available public lavatories than any other major North American city."[8] Such a policy would be in line with a strategy that can be observed in many other cites: the increasing privatization of restroom facilities across extensive stretches of urban space. The only available lavatories are often those within businesses, restaurants, office high rises, and other at least quasi-public spaces that can be selective about access, for example, limiting usage to "paying customers."

Thus, in many of these examples, it is not simply the case that a technology that had been open to multiple stable uses is now restrictively redesigned to close off one usage. Sometimes instead the entire device is eliminated or an area is completely shut off to everyone. It's modification as removal, inscription as erasure.

8. Davis 1990, 234.

4. Politics

CITIES ENACT ORDINANCES that target the behaviors of people living unhoused. Seemingly every aspect of daily life is subject to legal scrutiny. There are laws against sleeping, sitting, and lying down in public (sometimes referred to as "sit/lie" laws).[1] There are laws against loitering and camping. It is often illegal to sleep in a car. Cities may outlaw pushing shopping carts or storing personal items in public space. Hygiene standards may be enforced by law. Panhandling is made a crime. Some cities even ban others from giving out food to unhoused people.

These kinds of laws are a crucial piece of our story. The central claim of this pamphlet is that design and law come together to unjustly and unethically push the unhoused out of shared public spaces. Homeless advocacy groups often point out that these laws do not have the effect of addressing the problem of homelessness but instead treat unhoused people as if they themselves are the problem. The threat of citation or arrest posed by laws like these forces unhoused people out of public areas and into the marginal spaces of the city. Antihomeless designs are often combined with these sorts of antihomeless laws to effectively remove the unhoused from view.

Although it is difficult to know whether antihomeless designs are being implemented by cities at an increasing rate, it is clear that many of these designs continue to be newly built and installed in cities across the globe. But in contrast, it is readily pos-

1. Some police departments will even develop practices to counter the strategy discussed in the introduction in which unhoused people spend time at bus stops to avoid antiloitering laws; officers monitor the stops and issue citations to anyone who lets too many busses go by.

sible to track the rate of the enactment of antihomeless laws. For example, the United States has seen a sharp increase over the past few years.[2]

Homeless advocates argue that laws such as those listed here amount to the criminalization of homelessness. When behaviors essential to an unhoused person's mere existence constitute the grounds for arrest, then homelessness itself has been made a crime. This means that for many cities, one of the chief strategies for addressing the problem of homelessness is the attempt to process unhoused people through the criminal justice system. We should ask ourselves whether it is a just practice to approach homelessness as criminal behavior. We should consider the morality of arresting unhoused people simply for being unhoused, keeping in mind the harassment of unwarranted arrest and the fact that a criminal record makes it harder to find employment.

These laws and designs enter into what could be called a politics of visibility. Insofar as antihomeless laws and designs are successful in pushing the unhoused out of public spaces, an effect is to make the problem of homelessness itself less visible to the larger community.[3] Many of the restrictionary design modifications under consideration here—the antisleep benches, the antipick garbage cans—are created with at least two things in mind: (1) prohibiting the usage preferred by some unhoused people and also (2) doing so without at the same time disrupting the smooth experience of the device in terms of its dominant usage. For example, antisleep features make it difficult to sleep on a bench while at the same time easy to sit. And they do these two things all while making it easy to overlook this very effort to prevent the sleep usage. That is, these designs make it easy to overlook the politics of the bench.

2. National Law Center on Homelessness and Poverty 2014.
3. These issues thus have connections to other projects in STS and the philosophy of technology that attempt to highlight the politics of people who go unseen. See esp. Casper and Moore 2009; Star 1990.

This combination of law and design can sometimes be so effective that it renders the entire problem of homelessness—and also the unhoused people themselves—invisible to others. This invisibility has the potential to lead the larger community to grow unaware of the problem or even to mistakenly assume that the problem is less severe than it actually is. If the problem of homelessness is never encountered in daily life, and nor are the mechanisms that drive away the unhoused, then it becomes easier never to think about the issue.

The unhoused are, almost by definition, an especially disenfranchised population and a vulnerable one, often stereotyped and scapegoated and often subject to the indifference or hostility of others in the community. But the unhoused do have at least some influence. They can organize politically, like anyone else, and establish allies. They can act as members of homeless advocacy groups. And the unhoused do maintain one important source of political capital within their everyday lives: their visibility. It is of course a fraught form of capital; being visibly unhoused can be dangerous and can draw unwanted attention from law enforcement. And the visibility of the problem of homelessness does not always call forth support from the larger community. Nevertheless, insofar as unhoused people are present in shared public spaces, the problem of homelessness is more difficult to forget about or ignore. Thus the combined strategy of implementing antihomeless law and antihomeless design yanks away this form of political influence.

Laws against panhandling are a paradigmatic example of these unethical and unjust dynamics. In public spaces, individuals should be free to speak to one another, within reasonable regulations against harassment and harm. Antipanhandling laws make it a crime to ask others for money. The particular ways such ordinances are written vary widely from city to city. Sometimes they outlaw "begging." Sometimes they are effective citywide; other times they apply only to specific areas. In most cases, these laws unfairly target this particular form of public speech. While anyone may inquire about the time of day, or ask if you've heard the good news about his religion, the act of requesting a charitable donation is singled out as criminal. The decision to make only this particular type of request a crime is often exclusively a response to the fact that some people are made uncomfortable by the experience of interacting with an unhoused person.

Critics of antipanhandling laws in the United States argue that they violate a right to free speech protected by the First Amendment of the Constitution. A request for a charitable donation, if done in a nonaggressive manner, is an example of speech that causes no harm and introduces no danger. Thus laws against panhandling unjustly take away basic rights. They are an illegal imposition of the will of a majority upon a disenfranchised minority of the citizenship. And the courts have increasingly begun to take notice. In a series of recent victories, panhandling bans have been overturned in cities such as Worchester, Massachusetts, Portland, Maine, and Grand Junction, Colorado.[4] This has incited cities across the United States to reevaluate and sometimes even suspend their own antipanhandling ordinances, as groups like the American Civil Liberties Union prepare more challenges. As Maria Foscarinis, executive director of the National Law Center on Homelessness and Poverty, puts it, "these decisions are important not only because they protect the speech rights of homeless people, but also because they have struck down a common tool used by local governments to criminalize homelessness."[5] However, the rate at which these laws have been overturned is dwarfed by the rate at which new laws banning panhandling have ballooned in recent years. Between

4. http://www.bostonglobe.com/metro/2015/11/10/federal-judge-strikes-down-worcester-panhandling-ordinances/8hPfcDVNCG2eQxR1D8trjL/story.html, http://www.pressherald.com/2015/09/11/portland-loses-appeal-of-court-ruling-that-allows-panhandling-on-street-medians/, http://www.coloradoindependent.com/155527/court-shoots-down-grand-junction-panhandling-ordinance.

5. Foscarinis 2015.

2011 and 2014, there was a 20 percent increase in the passage of laws in the United States that ban panhandling in particular places, lifting the total to more than 75 percent of cities surveyed.[6]

Sometimes antipanhandling ordinances are couched as outlawing only "aggressive" panhandling. This may seem at first to be a compassionate and pragmatic solution: regular, nonthreatening panhandling is permitted, but panhandling is outlawed when it is threatening or otherwise deemed invasively persistent. The problem here is that bans on aggressive panhandling lend themselves to unjust overreach. They put legal forms of panhandling under unwarranted scrutiny and pressure. And they give overaggressive law enforcement officers a tool to harass legal panhandlers. This is reflected in the fact that most aggressive panhandling bans are redundant. Cities tend already to regulate forms of aggressive behavior with laws against harassment or disrupting the peace or with broad laws against disorderly conduct, so aggressive panhandling bans may have only the unjust effect of discouraging legal panhandling (something which should otherwise be understood as protected speech).

The political implications of antihomeless design force us to expand our conception of technological "guilt." The precise manner in which a technology is articulated—both in terms of our linguistic descriptions and in terms of material inscriptions—is connected to our society's systems of law, representation, economics, and criminal justice. As Donna Haraway puts it, "this is what articulation does; it is always noninnocent, contested practice; the partners are never set once and for all. . . . Articulation is work, and it may fail. All the people who care, cognitively, emotionally, and politically, must articulate their position in a field constrained by a new collective entity."[7] Through social theory, and in particular here through actor-network theory, we have found ways to think

6. National Law Center for Homelessness and Poverty 2014.

7. Haraway 2004, 91.

about technology's social character. But within the issues emerging around antihomeless law, we see that technologies like the antisleep bench or antipick garbage can are implicated not only in social networks but also in larger political structures.[8] That is, rather than being understood as taking part only in particular group agendas, technologies should also be understood as essentially wrapped up within our society's larger politics, including economic systems, law enforcement procedures, democratic and undemocratic representational schemes, penal methods, and racial and sexual power dynamics, to name just a few of the basics.

Here again it is important to interrogate the intuitions that may linger in the backs of our minds—possibly without our explicit awareness—about how technology changes our world. We must remain careful not to fall into a supposition, on one hand, that technology is somehow always politically innocent and, on the other (and sometimes at the same time, despite contradictions), that technology is inherently forward moving, problem solving, and beneficial. On these political dimensions, the philosopher of technology Andrew Feenberg's work is instructive. He articulates how technologies have the potential both to challenge prevailing structures of power and also to reinforce them.

Feenberg explains that because technologies are always multistable, "there is no unique correlation between technological advance and the distribution of social power."[9] He distinguishes between two potential effects of technological advance. One possibility is that the new technologies "conserve" the existing "hierarchy." He writes, "social hierarchies can generally be preserved and reproduced as new technology is introduced."[10] Another, more

8. The inability of STS perspectives to account fully for technology's larger political (and not just social) implications has perhaps been best articulated in Winner (1993).

9. Feenberg 1999, 76. Feenberg does not use the term multistability but instead a conception of technology's ambivalence. For the specific purposes of the argument of this pamphlet, we can consider the two equivalent.

10. Ibid., 76.

"democratic" possibility is that technological advance challenges the prevailing political structures and social norms that have kept some in power over others. On this alternative possibility, he writes, "new technology can also be used to undermine the existing social hierarchy or to force it to meet needs it has ignored." This possibility is reflected in "the technical initiatives that often accompany the structural reforms pursued by union, environmental, and other social movements."[11]

This conception of technology helps to articulate the political danger of the instrumental, utopian, and dystopian attitudes. In its own way, each of these attitudes can discourage positive political action that could challenge traditional hierarchies. Because they assume that technologies control our destiny, determinist attitudes like utopianism and dystopianism can disincline toward working for political change. For example, if you are a committed dystopian, and you think that technological advance necessarily leads us toward some grim future, then you might see political action to be pointless. The best we can do is inveigh impotently against the unstoppable march of technology, with political progress possible only through the abandonment of technological development altogether. If you are a utopian, then you might be even more disinclined toward political intervention. That is, if you assume that technological advance is inherently good, then you may see no reason to establish political checks on its development. Even more, you may assume that our current problems—environmental degradation, world hunger, you name it—do not require political solutions at all; technology will fix everything soon enough.

From Feenberg's perspective, this is dangerously naive. Sure, technologies have brought undeniably positive and life-changing advances to medicine, transportation, and so on. But it is a political (and empirical) mistake to assume that these advances will always be accrued equally and democratically, or even fairly. And, owing to

11. Ibid.

the multiple stable paths forward possible for any technology, it is a mistake to assume that technological advance itself will correct for inequity. That is, it is a mistake to assume that technological advance will always solve—rather than contribute to—our problems, especially the problems of the disadvantaged and the less wealthy. It certainly has not always done so in the past. If things remain on their current political course, Feenberg argues, then technological advance will simply continue to reinforce hierarchies.

These dynamics are most straightforward in the case of the instrumentalist attitude. If you think technologies are always socially and politically neutral, if you think they are inherently innocent, then you might mistakenly believe that they cannot possibly contribute to the agendas that keep some advantaged and others disadvantaged. Instrumentalists often agree that, sure, people oppress one another all the time in loathsome ways. But, in this view, technologies themselves are never implicated. If technologies are nonpolitical by definition, then they cannot take part in oppressive politics, nor can they ever have the potential to challenge oppression. That is, an instrumentalist may fail to see the possibility for positive democratic change through technological development and may remain blind to the ways that technologies actively maintain societal hierarchies.

To be certain, it may be possible to develop utopian, dystopian, and instrumental accounts of technological advance that are sophisticated enough to somehow also appreciate technological multistability. This pamphlet isn't a veiled attack on some particular philosophy out there. The point is that we all should keep an eye on those attitudes regarding technological development that are pervasive across society and that may linger to differing degrees in the recesses of our individual minds. Even if we are not explicitly committed to any of these positions, these utopian, dystopian, and instrumentalist attitudes can influence us at unexpected times and incline us against acting for positive political change.

I suggest that antihomeless design is a case-in-point example of technological development that works to conserve societal hierarchies. Through their strategic combination with the system of antihomeless laws, antihomeless technologies serve the interests of the already powerful and work to further subjugate the already disadvantaged. More specifically, antihomeless designs like the antisleep bench or the antipick garbage can and antihomeless laws like those against loitering or panhandling serve a city's prevailing social and business interests, while simultaneously running counter to the interests of the unhoused population. To put it all together, antihomeless design and law reinforce hierarchies by catering to the business class at the expense of the just treatment of unhoused people as fellow citizens and the moral treatment of unhoused people as human beings.

The roles of antihomeless technologies in conserving hierarchies become clearer in their connection to antihomeless laws and the politics of visibility. Taken alone, a single antisleep bench, if its restrictionary intentions are noticed at all, may appear only to discourage someone from sleeping in one particular spot. To recognize the bench's larger political significance, it must be analyzed in terms of the system of related antihomeless laws and the pattern of antihomeless design installations across public space. Antihomeless design can become policy.

One place to look for evidence of this is in the design guidelines and best practice recommendations of our cities' public transit authorities. For example, Winnipeg Transit's design guidelines for sustainable transportation states,

> If the bus stop is located in an area where there is a possibility of people using the seating for sleeping or loitering, the seat should be divided by an arm rest, planter or other form of divider so that the space is not long enough for someone to lay down on.

The Riverside Transit Agency, which serves parts of southern California, writes in its bus stop guidelines that "benches should have anti-vagrant bars or another deterrent as part of the design." Or as the Greater Vancouver Transportation Authority's guidelines summarize the whole issue, "benches without middle armrests are preferred, unless sleeping on benches is an issue."[12] That single bench, then, should be understood not only to make it difficult to sleep in one specific area but to contribute to a larger effort set forth systematically in policy, and incorporated into design, to coerce the unhoused out of public space.

Gender is an example of a political dimension across which we can see varying statistics on homelessness. The majority of unhoused people are male, making up 60 percent of the adult "homeless" population in the United States, and 70 percent of those who remain unsheltered. A specific cause of homelessness faced by women in particular is domestic violence. Cities in the United States routinely list domestic violence among their major causes of homelessness. The annual census report conducted by the National Network to End Domestic Violence finds that of all the unmet requests made to domestic violence service programs, more than half (and in most years, more than 60 percent) are for housing.[13] According to a study by the Williams Institute, a massively disproportionate number of youths living unhoused in the United States are lesbian, gay, bisexual, or transgender (LGBT). Around 40 percent of those served by homeless youth organizations identify as LGBT, despite making up only 7 percent of the youth population generally.[14]

Another example of a salient political structure that cuts across the issue of homelessness is race. Which racial groups make up the largest proportions of the homeless population will of course

12. Winnipeg Transit 2006, 29; Riverside Transportation Agency 2015, 6.5; Greater Vancouver Transit Authority 2007, 63.

13. The statistics on the gender of homeless people in the United States come from the 2015 HUD report at https://www.hudexchange.info /resources/documents/2015-AHAR-Part-1.pdf. The point that U.S. cities report domestic violence as a major cause of homelessness can be found in the annual "Status Report on Hunger and Homelessness" compiled by the U.S. Conference of Mayors. For the 2015 report, see https://www.usmayors .org/pressreleases/uploads/2015/1221-report-hhreport.pdf. The National Network to End Domestic Violence conducts an annual census report. For their archive, see http://nnedv.org/projects/census.html.

14. Durso and Gates 2012.

vary widely country to country, state by state in the United States, and region by region within those places. Still, the data on the racial makeup of homelessness are revealing. In the United States, African Americans represent an outsized portion of the overall homeless population, making up 40 percent of the national homeless total, compared to representing 13.3 percent of the country's total population. The same can be said for Native Americans, who comprise 1.3 percent of the country's total population but 2.7 percent of its homeless.[15]

The Coalition for the Homeless reports similarly eye-popping numbers in its study of the shelter system in New York City, whose occupancy has seen all-time records in recent years. Whereas 1 in every 72 residents of the city made use of the shelter system at least once over the course of 2014, that number drops to 1 in 294 white people and jumps up to 1 in 28 African Americans.[16] The racial dynamics are different in the state of Hawaii, where the problem of homelessness has gotten so out of hand that, at the time of this writing, the governor has declared a state of emergency over the issue. Where indigenous people comprise 10.2 percent of the total state population, they make up an astounding 39 percent of

15. For information on the total U.S. population, see https://www.census.gov/quickfacts/fact/table/US/PST045216 . For information on the racial makeup of the U.S. homeless population, see http://www.hudexchange.info/resources/documents/2015-AHAR-Part-1.pdf. As a point of comparison, "Hispanics or Latinos" make up 20 percent of the national homeless population—compared to 17 percent of the total U.S. population. (The Hispanic category in census data is tabulated as an "ethnicity" rather than a "race" and operates independently of racial categories like white and African American. So the Hispanics or Latinos of this group may identify with either of these, and other, racial categories.) White people—including both those who identify as Hispanic and those who do not—make up 49 percent of the national homeless total. This same group makes up 77 percent of the total U.S. population.

16. http://www.coalitionforthehomeless.org/wp-content/uploads/2015/03/SOTH2015.pdf; http://bigstory.ap.org/article/8838714511984c00ab8d448bfa188293/hawaii-governor-declares-state-emergency-homelessness.

the state's total number counted as "homeless" and fully half of all those living unsheltered.[17]

Any number of large-scale political factors could contribute to the racial disparities seen in unhoused populations in different cities, states, and regions, including well-documented phenomena such as housing discrimination and job application discrimination, segregation, and the inequities of schooling, health care, inherited wealth, and opportunity. When unhoused people spend time, camp, and panhandle in popular downtown and business districts, this can represent a breakdown of long-standing class and racial segregation. It seems possible that part of the appeal of antihomeless laws and designs that push the unhoused out of such districts is that they cater to the prejudices of shoppers, tourists, and office workers unaccustomed to that breakdown in segregation. Whatever the different causes of these disparities in different areas, part of the point of spotlighting the racial dynamics of homelessness here is to emphasize one deeply political aspect of the problem. The problem of homelessness thus does not reduce to mere social conflicts between this and that group but also includes the history of racism in the United States. When cities pass laws and build public-space technologies that discriminate against the unhoused, they play a part in this continuing history.

One of the things that is revealed when thinking about the political dimensions of public-space technologies is that "the public" is itself a contested concept. Who counts as a member of the public for whom public spaces are designed? Should the unhoused also count, even if they are not a constituency for which politicians normally take a stand? Because they are especially in need and especially vulnerable, should the unhoused be considered greater

17. For the percentage of "Native Hawaiian and Other Pacific Islander alone" in the total Hawaiian population, see https://www.census.gov/quickfacts/fact/table/HI,US/PST045216. For the racial makeup of the homeless population of Hawaii, see https://www.hudexchange.info/resource/reportmanagement/published/CoC_PopSub_State_HI_2015.pdf.

stakeholders in public-space designs? What the public "should" mean and what we "ought" to do about it are open moral and political questions. Insofar as we are increasingly installing antihomeless designs and instituting antihomeless laws, we are already answering these questions in practice and shutting the unhoused out of consideration.

Interlude: Cruelty

In 2009, a challenge was issued to local ordinances in the city of Boise, Idaho, that outlaw sleeping in public spaces. The plaintiffs in the case were themselves living unhoused when convicted of violating these laws. They argued that laws against camping and sleeping in public make it a crime to be homeless. The number of unhoused people in cities like Boise at times exceeds the space available in shelters. Thus these kinds of laws punish those left with no other option. The plaintiffs claimed that their rights are infringed upon whenever the Boise Police Department enforces these rules.

In August 2015, the Obama administration's Department of Justice (DOJ) stepped in to register its own interpretation, thus launching the case into national attention.[18] The DOJ came down in favor of the plaintiffs. In a statement of interest, the DOJ wrote, "In those circumstances enforcement of the ordinances amounts to the criminalization of homelessness, in violation of the Eighth Amendment."[19] On the basis of this reasoning (and other legal precedent), the DOJ's claim is that the criminal prosecution of those who sleep outside when faced without an available alternative constitutes a violation of their constitutional protection against cruel and unusual punishment.

But then in a stunning turn, in September 2015, the judge threw out the case. As the *Idaho Statesman* reports, Judge Ronald E.

---

18. Rosenberger 2015.
19. http://www.justice.gov/opa/file/643766/download.

Bush dismissed the suit under the reasoning that the particular plaintiffs had not demonstrated that an imminent threat has been placed upon themselves personally.[20] This is in part because many of the plaintiffs are no longer living unhoused. And although camping citations in Boise have spiked over the last few years, the judge saw no specific evidence that any have been issued in an instance when shelter space was unavailable.[21]

The Boise Mayor's Office appeared eager to put the case in the rearview mirror, stating,

> We agree with and are very pleased by the court's decision to dismiss this lawsuit. Our efforts on behalf of those in our community who are experiencing homelessness are concrete. Now, with this case behind us, we will be able to better focus on creating positive gains against this challenging societal problem.[22]

This seems hasty. As Judge Bush himself notes, there is no reason that other, more eligible plaintiffs could not file the same exact suit.

Stepping back, we should recognize the importance of the statement issued by the DOJ: it does more than simply weigh in on the Boise case; it presents cities across the United States with a legal test. And it presents us all with a test of our moral intuitions.

The legal test is straightforward enough. Municipalities across America have been issued fair warning: according to the 2015 statement, the DOJ views any law that prohibits sleeping or camping in public when alternatives are unavailable to violate the U.S. Constitution. Multiple news outlets report that their respective cities are now reexamining their anticamping laws, with some already making changes.

Research provided by the National Law Center on Homelessness and Poverty is helpful for understanding the scope of the implica-

20. Sewell 2015.

21. Wright and Associated Press 2015.

22. http://mayor.cityofboise.org/news-releases/2015/09/mayor-bieter
-statement-on-dismissal-of-bell-v-city-of-boise/.

tions of the DOJ's position. In a report on laws targeting the un-housed, the center analyzes a sample of 187 U.S. cities.[23] More than half are found to prohibit camping in at least some public areas. More than one-third maintain citywide camping bans. And more than half prohibit sitting or lying down in certain areas. This reflects a significant national increase in the enactment of such camping and sit/lie laws over the past few years.

We can extend the logic of the DOJ's statement to consider whether there are other ways that anticamping laws could violate the Eighth Amendment. For example, we should consider whether it is an example of cruel and unusual punishment to criminally prosecute someone for sleeping outside when issues like mental illness or addiction make it difficult for this person to find shelter.

What about when people are turned away by the local shelter for reasons other than capacity? They might be denied entrance because of substance usage or because they have pets. Maybe the reason they opt not to use the shelter is because they do not want to participate in mandatory religious services. Maybe they have reached a maximum stay limit. For many, the timetables (by which you must arrive, eat, etc.) are too demanding, possibly conflicting with working hours. For others, the lack of privacy, and sometimes the lack of safety, is enough to keep them out of the shelter system. Because the availability of shelter space has become the basis of the very constitutionality of anticamping laws, shelter rules take on weighty legal and moral implications.

Judge Bush makes exactly these points in his suggestion that the Boise suit could be raised again. He says,

> There may, for instance, be an individual with a mental or physical condition that has interfered with [his] or her ability to seek access to or stay at shelters, with such difficulties likely to continue in the future. Or, perhaps a homeless individual will refuse to stay at the River of Life and can support a claim that the facility requires par-

23. National Law Center on Homelessness and Poverty 2014.

ticipation in religious practices for homeless individuals to stay in temporary housing there.[24]

We could additionally consider the cruelty of prosecuting those whose status as unhoused has been imposed by a lack of employment opportunities or affordable housing. In all of these cases, there is at least an argument to be made that it may be cruel and unusual to punish someone for sleeping outside.

We could extend the DOJ's logic even further and widen the scope of the kinds of laws under evaluation. Do other antihomeless laws, in addition to camping bans, violate a citizen's constitutional protection against cruel and unusual punishment? Take, for example, laws that enforce hygiene standards. If factors like shelter capacity and the unavailability of public showering amenities make it impossible for an unhoused person to stay clean, then it may be cruel to make it a crime to fail to meet certain sanitary minimums. The same could even be said about the availability of public restrooms. Cities will sometimes eliminate public restroom facilities in part as an attempt to ward off the unhoused. If unhoused people have no other option, then laws against public urination appear to punish them for something unavoidable.

The DOJ's statement also presents a test of our moral intuitions. It prompts us to consider what "cruelty" means with regard to our treatment of those living unhoused. Beyond questions of the constitutionality of criminalizing homelessness, we can ask when exactly a city's actions toward unhoused people should be considered morally cruel. With the DOJ's statement in mind, we can consider whether it is morally cruel to persecute the unhoused when they are faced with few other options.

Under this lens, we can reexamine any of the laws and designs we've considered so far. When unhoused people are faced with a lack of alternatives, then it appears morally cruel to criminalize behaviors like using a shopping cart, storing private items in

24. Sewell 2015.

public space, loitering, or panhandling. Bring to mind again the array of antihomeless designs we have been investigating, such as antisleep benches, ledge spikes, fences, and antipick garbage cans. If it is morally cruel to criminalize the act of sleeping in public, then there is correspondingly cruelty in the concerted effort made by cities to design the objects of our world specifically to push the unhoused population out of our shared public space.

Thus, far from applying only to the Boise case, the DOJ's statement prods us to consider the legal and moral cruelty beneath these aspects of our cities' approaches to the problem of homelessness. It spotlights in particular the way that the anticamping ordinances of many American cities violate the Constitution. And more generally, it points out cruelties all around us, set in laws that unjustly target unhoused people and built callously into the objects of our public spaces.

5. Occlusion

CONSIDER AGAIN the experience of someone sitting on a bench at a bus stop. Imagine that this person waits at this same bus stop each morning as part of a daily commute and today is a day like any other. Imagine as well that the bus stop has been built with some of the antihomeless designs we've reviewed. The bench has been fit with partitions that discourage sleeping. Beside the bench is a small garbage can constructed in such a way that it discourages picking. Imagine that the commuter in our example is not herself living unhoused and rarely, if ever, thinks about things like trash picking, sleeping on benches, or navigating antiloitering ordinances.

Despite using this bus stop every day, it is possible that this person will at most times be barely—if at all—aware of the antihomeless agenda built into this setting. In fact, one reason this person may not notice the politics of this situation is exactly because it is all so routine. The utter normalcy of the experience itself keeps the politics occluded from view. In this way, there is a political dimension to what gets noticed and what goes unseen. There is a politics to perception itself. We can turn again to the philosophy of technology to help develop what could be called a phenomenology of political occlusion.

Phenomenology excels at providing deep descriptions of our experience of the everyday world and following out the philosophical implications. One fundamental contribution is Martin Heidegger's account of "tool use." Heidegger considers the experience of someone using a hammer. He writes, "The less we just stare at the hammer-Thing, and the more we seize hold of it and use it, the more primordial does our relationship to it become, and

the more unveiledly is it encountered as that which it is—as equipment."[1] What he's saying here, at least in part, is that when someone is using a hammer and is engrossed in hammering, the thing
that is most present to this person is not the hammer itself but the
work being done. Heidegger follows this example further and considers what happens when the hammer suddenly breaks in the user's hand, what is sometimes referred to in this literature as technological "breakdown." In such an event, the hammer would be
once again experienced as a significant presence, an object, in this
case now a broken object that stands in the way of the work that
had been getting done just a moment ago. Where the hammer in
use is barely present in this experience at all, the broken hammer
instead itself stands forward, and this person now has a more explicit awareness of its meaning and its various associations, such
as the nails and workbench, all sitting there unable to be used.

Another fundamental contribution to phenomenological
thought is Maurice Merleau-Ponty's description of bodily experience. Whereas Heidegger's account of tool use had centered on
presence, Merleau-Ponty explores the bodily aspects of technology usage. As we go on about our day, and as we grow accustomed
to our surroundings and to the technologies we commonly use, we
develop bodily perceptual habits. Our bodily awareness is subject
to change and can become altered and extended across the technologies we use. As Merleau-Ponty puts it, "habit expresses the

---

1. Heidegger 2000, 98. Heidegger aficionados may be dismayed that
I do not go into further detail on his technical terminology, for example,
referring to the hammer in use as "ready-to-hand" and the broken hammer
as "present-to-hand." But the reason I do not delve more deeply into
Heidegger's philosophy here is that I do not wish to commit the ideas of
this pamphlet to his particular metaphysics. Ultimately, Heidegger can be
understood to offer a foundational account of the nature of being itself, a
distinctive critique of the history of Western metaphysics. Here, instead
committed to a postphenomenological framework (see chapter 1, note 4), I
am attempting to develop a pragmatic account of human–technology relations. Don Ihde's example of the multistability of hammers in chapter 1 is a
not-too-subtle dig at Heidegger's allegedly totalizing metaphysical account.

power we have of dilating our being in the world, or of altering our existence through the incorporation of instruments."[2] We live through our habits. They prime our perception and shape our bodily awareness. And we experience normal technology usage through bodily habituation.

Merleau-Ponty gives the example of using a typewriter. He writes, "Knowing how to type, then, is not the same as knowing the location of each letter on the keyboard, nor even having acquired a conditioned reflex for each key that is triggered upon seeing it."[3] Like the hammerer who thinks about the work and not the hammer itself, someone typing thinks about the content of what he is writing and not about each individual keystroke. Only someone still brand-new to typing will be preoccupied by his own fingers and the arrangement of the keys. Merleau-Ponty continues, "The subject who learns to type literally incorporates the space of the keyboard into his bodily space." Through learned habituation, a person's bodily awareness can be understood to extend through the keyboard.

Following Merleau-Ponty, Don Ihde refers to this as our capacity to "embody" technology. When we become accustomed to embodying a technology, it takes on a kind of experiential "transparency." Ihde says that when it comes to our technologies, we have a "double desire that, on one side, is a wish for total transparency, total embodiment, for the technology to truly 'become me.' . . . The other side is the desire to have the power, the transformation that the technology makes available."[4] Our technologies sometimes greatly change our abilities and our experience. Yet through our design practices, and through the ways we as users become acclimated to our devices, we may in many moments remain barely aware of those changes and, indeed, sometimes barely aware of the device itself.

2. Merleau-Ponty 1945, 145.
3. Ibid.
4. Ihde 1990, 75.

My suggestion is that these aspects of learned bodily habituation are a crucial part of political occlusion. We can come to overlook the politics of our technologies and our surroundings as we develop habits of perception. Despite using the bus stop each day, our commuter does not need to think consciously about the bus stop itself very often. Indeed, it is exactly because the bus stop is used routinely that its specifics can go unnoticed. If, through long-developed perceptual habits, our commuter is not noticing the bench or garbage can, then this person is also not noticing the politics of antihomeless design built into those devices. And as we've noted, antisleep benches and antipick cans are designed so that the dominant "sitting" and "garbage depositing" usages remain easy and uninterrupted. My contention is that antihomeless politics in particular, and other political aspects of our technologies and our environment more generally, can become occluded within the normal bodily perceptual habits that we develop with our technologies and our material surroundings.

Contemporary theorist Linda Martín Alcoff notes that despite the fact that our perception itself is deeply set with politics, we are not helpless in these matters. She writes, "Perceptual practices are dynamic even when congealed into habit, and that dynamism can be activated by the existence of multiple forms of the gaze in various cultural productions and by the challenge of contradictory perceptions."[5] Put into some of the vocabulary reviewed earlier, part of her point here is that it is possible to experience a kind of perceptual breakdown, one that can help to disrupt the habits of our everyday perception and call attention to them. Like the way the breakdown of the hammer shatters its experiential transparency, making it an explicit object of attention and revealing its associations, perhaps we can similarly attempt to draw out the occluded political associations of our built environment. This could help us to evaluate the politics of how we see the world and also the politics of what we

5. Alcoff 2006, 189.

have learned to fail to see. Alcoff continues, "To put it simply, people are capable of change. Merleau-Ponty's analysis helps us to provide a more accurate understanding of where—that is, at what level of experience—change needs to occur."[6]

What would it mean to break the habits of our relations to anti-homeless design? We can imagine instances in which the bus stop bench fails to function as expected in its dominant sitting affordance because of an antihomeless feature. Perhaps one day our daily commuter is wearing a big backpack, or holding a child, or lugging a grocery bag, and a bench divider makes it difficult to sit. Maybe this person watches someone else inconvenienced by the dividers, such as someone with a physical disability. Perhaps this person accidentally drops something into the garbage can and then has trouble retrieving it because of an antipick measure. These experiences may alert this person to the presence of the antihomeless design features around him, and such a realization might make him consider the political implications. That is, these moments of breakdown might disrupt habits of everyday perception and reveal the bus stop's normally unnoticed political dimensions.

Perhaps instead it is the presence of someone living unhoused that breaks these perceptual habits. Maybe an unhoused person attempts awkwardly to rest on the bench despite its antisleep design, and this awakens our daily commuter to the surrounding politics. I have often suspected that one of the things that makes panhandling such a striking experience for the person being panhandled is its breakdown character—an encounter with a panhandler doesn't simply present someone with an instance of homelessness; it breaks down the everyday habitual forgetting about the entire problem and, indeed, about the politics of our everyday surroundings in general. Perhaps our commuter watches an unhoused person being harassed at the bus stop by the police. Maybe our commuter talks with this person about the experience.

6. Ibid.

This brings us to the epistemological aspect of political occlusion. Part of what may prevent us from seeing the politics built into the world around us is the basic fact that we are each limited by our own personal history of experience. We may not notice the politics of our built environment because we have never learned to look for them. We don't know that we don't know what we don't know; and what we don't know, we're not prepared to see.

We can turn to feminist standpoint theory for insight into how this works. A central idea in this line of thinking is that each person perceives the world from his own epistemological standpoint. That means that what each person knows is limited by the fact that she is an individual body in the world with a particular vantage point and a particular restricted set of life experiences. Any community will have limits on its perspective, and the dominant community will have its own pervading biases, biases that could be involved in the practices that contribute to the marginalization of those less advantaged groups. As Patricia Hill Collins explains, "in brief, insiders have undergone similar experiences, possess a common history, and share taken-for-granted knowledge that characterizes 'thinking as usual.'"[7] The dominant community will remain largely unaware of these biases, even as it benefits from them.

Standpoint theory goes further to claim that these biases can be routed out by incorporating marginalized people into the dominant conversation. The point is not that those in marginalized societal positions have a better view of the truth; all standpoints are limited and, as such, are inherently biased. But because they are specifically disadvantaged by the biases of the dominant perspective, these marginalized positions do have a special vantage point on exactly those biases, a vantage point that the dominant position distinctly lacks. This is in part what Alcoff is talking about in the preceding quotation in which she urges us to bring together "the

7. Collins 1986, S25–S26.

existence of multiple forms of the gaze in various cultural productions."[8] We have a lot to learn from one another precisely because we come from different limited perspectives, and the dominant perspective in particular can learn about its own biases through conversation with the people who are marginalized by those biases. Sandra Harding goes so far as to claim that including the perspectives of marginalized people has the potential to make the dominant discussion more objective. She writes, "In order to gain a causal critical view of the interests and values that constitute the dominant conceptual projects, one must start one's thought, one's research project, from outside those conceptual schemes and the activities that generate them; one must start from the lives excluded as origins of their designs—from 'marginal lives.'"[9]

We can bring these insights from feminist standpoint theory into our account of technological multistability, perceptual habit, and political occlusion. Insofar as one belongs to the dominant community, one will often take up technologies in terms of their dominant stability. We see this in our example of the commuter who uses the bus stop in its dominant stability, the stability for which the bus stop was designed and installed. And through normal usage, this commuter has developed perceptual habits with regard to the dominant stability, barely noticing most features of the bus stop as he travels each day.

This commuter's experience living through the dominant standpoint is set within bodily perceptual habit. The unhoused are an example of a marginalized standpoint in this case, disadvantaged by the bus stop designs and the larger network of antihomeless design and policy. Our commuter goes about a normal day unaware of these dynamics, these politics occluded from view by the limits of his life experiences, by the normalcy of the experience set within perceptual habit, and by the effectiveness of the design that has

8. Alcoff 2006, 189.
9. Harding 1995, 342.

pushed the problem of homelessness from view. But this could be changed if this person were to interact with and take seriously the experiences of unhoused people. And this could be changed if the dominant perspective itself were to be transformed. This would involve a change to what is widely considered normal. It would involve turning to the marginalized people themselves, unhoused people, to learn about their experiences.

The antidote to political occlusion can thus involve more than simply waiting around for Heideggerian breakdown. It can involve taking seriously the experiences of those who are systematically disadvantaged and otherwise typically ignored.

Interlude: Farce

Artist Sean Godsell has designed a bench that transforms into a covered shelter. The plank where one would normally sit can be lifted up to reveal another fixed plank underneath. The upper plank is attached to the fixed plank by a hinge, so it can be lifted to create a space under it. Rods can be used to keep the upper plank in place as a kind of roof. Thus, someone who would like to sleep on the bench can unfold it into a kind of sheltered bed.[10]

The work of Godsell and others can be understood as a form of protest art. It has the potential to raise consciousness on issues of homelessness and public-space design and point creatively toward new possibilities. In can thus be broadly understood as a kind of "unrestrictionary" modification, that is, one that counters a restrictionary feature, making formerly "closed-off" possibilities for usage available once more. Perhaps the most straightforward example would be if someone were to forcibly remove an armrest to make an antisleep bench once again into something on which a person could lie down. Whereas the armrest or seat partition is an example of a restrictionary modification that closes off a stability

10. http://www.seangodsell.com/park-bench-house.

of a multistable technology, the forcible removal of the antisleep feature works to "reopen" that stability. Consciousness-raising artwork can also be a part of unrestrictionary efforts, working to call out restrictionary designs, advocate against them, and offer alternatives.

Design theorist Carl DiSalvo looks at technology through a political perspective called *agonism,* which understands democracy always to involve disagreement. He explains, "For democracy to flourish, spaces of confrontation must exist, and contestation must occur."[11] DiSalvo claims that this disagreement occurs not only through verbal and written argumentation, debate, and protest but also through design. He uses the term *adversarial design* to refer to objects, products, services, and other things made specifically to challenge prevailing political forces. He writes that designs are adversarial when they "enact the political conditions of contemporary society and function as contestational objects that challenge and offer alternatives to dominant practices and agendas."[12] I suggest that the line of protest art that criticizes antihomeless design is a useful example of this idea.

As discussed previously, it can be easy for the politics of our everyday world to go unnoticed. We can connect these art projects with the ideas of the previous chapter, in which we considered the phenomenological dimensions of occluded politics. Insofar as the dominant perspective fails to notice the pervasive antihomeless agenda set in policy and design, and insofar as that failure to notice is embodied in our habits of perception, these kinds of adversarial art projects have the potential to incite a kind of perceptual breakdown. By calling attention to otherwise often unnoticed antihomeless designs, by highlighting the unchosen possibilities for the design of public space, and by spotlighting their politics, these kinds of artworks challenge the antihomeless agenda.

11. DiSalvo 2012, 5.
12. Ibid., 115.

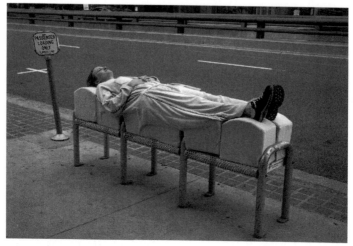

Figure 8. An Archisuit designed so that the wearer can lie down on an antisleep bench.
Courtesy of Sarah Ross.

Take the Archisuit project. Sarah Ross has designed a series of bodysuits called Archisuits, each fit with large and oddly shaped foam pieces attached to the wearer's back. Each suit calls out different antihomeless designs by revealing what strange and elaborate outfits would be required to lie, sit, or otherwise rest on a variety of common surfaces, including slopes, thin ledges, and antisleep bench designs.[13]

Another example is Michael Rackowitz's paraSITE designs. Each paraSITE is a custom-made inflatable tent. Every unit is specially built to attach to a particular building's heated air exhaust vent. The warm air simultaneously keeps the tent inflated and creates a warm, livable space inside.[14]

There's also the Pay & Sit bench, an incisive design satire created by Fabian Brunsing. When not in use, the Pay & Sit bench

13. http://www.insecurespaces.net/archisuits.html.
14. http://www.michaelrakowitz.com/parasite/.

Figure 9. The Pay & Sit coin-operated park bench. Courtesy of Fabian Brunsing.

features a series of sharp spikes poking upward from the sitting surface, reminiscent of the kinds of antihomeless spikes sometimes found on ledges. The device is coin operated. When money is inserted, the spikes retract into the bench for a set amount of time. A noise sounds when that time is almost up to warn the sitter to stand before the spikes reemerge. The Pay & Sit bench thus calls attention to a number of themes of contemporary public spaces, including their increasing regulation, the way this regulation is delegated to hostile architecture, and the increasingly pervasive strategy of excluding the riffraff with an entrance fee (such as in the privatization of public restrooms).[15]

Although the claims have been difficult to confirm, a number of news outlets report a wicked irony: inspired by Brunsing's model, a city in China has installed coin-operated and spike-studded benches of exactly this design in one of its parks.[16] If this is so, then the development of this device has progressed from ironic commentary to chillingly sincere implementation; first as farce, then as tragedy.

15. http://www.fabianbrunsing.de/.

16. http://www.npr.org/templates/story/story.php?storyId=129785015.

6. Opening Up

WHEN MOVIES WANT TO CONVEY the idea that it's a hot summer day in the city, they often include a shot of a fire hydrant blasting a torrent of water into the street, children playing in the spray. Fire hydrants thus present yet another example of a multistable public-space technology.[1] The dominant stability, the most common usage and in this case the purpose for which the hydrants are designed and installed, is their role in fighting fires. They, of course, are used as a water access point for firefighters to attach their hoses, with units spaced out across the city. The use of the hydrant as a way to cool off on a hot day is an iconic alternative stability.

Hydrants maintain multiple additional stabilities. We all know their role in the lives of passing dogs. They are at times tapped to refill street sweepers and other city cleaning equipment. Private businesses can contract with the city to utilize hydrants as a water source for construction projects. The "outlet cap" is the lid that covers over the spout where the hose is attached, and these caps are subject to theft. (This is evidenced by the fact that a chain often secures the cap to the base and that manufacturers offer caps composed of substances with no scrap value.) Police departments access fire hydrants to fuel water cannons used in riot control.

After all the examples of social and political conflicts over public-space technologies reviewed in the previous chapters, it should come as no surprise that similar struggles also play out over hydrants. The practice of using fire hydrants as a source of cool water in the summer is both complex and fraught. In New York City, for example, an open hydrant blasts more than one

1. Rosenberger 2017a.

thousand gallons of water into the street per minute.[2] This is wasteful and expensive. It can reduce the water pressure going to other fire hydrants. And the force of the water from an uncapped hydrant can also be dangerous to smaller children. But for poor neighborhoods, in which public pools may be rare, and where indoor air-conditioning may be unavailable, there may be no other options for avoiding the heat.

To prevent unapproved usage of fire hydrants, cities adopt both legal and design strategies. Continuing with the example of New York City, someone caught opening a fire hydrant in an unauthorized manner faces up to $1,000 in fines or up to thirty days' jail time. In conjunction with these kinds of policies, cities sometimes adopt hydrant designs that place limitations on how water can be accessed and, importantly, on who can gain access. Put in the terminology of actor-network theory, city governments and water companies will at times delegate to hydrant designs themselves the task of limiting who is allowed to operate a fire hydrant. Put in the terminology advanced in this pamphlet, hydrants can be conceived as multistable technologies with both firefighting and summer cooling stabilities. And hydrant redesigns that place limitations on who can use them can be conceived as restrictionary modifications. Such designs attempt to prohibit hydrant usage in terms of specific alternative stabilities, while continuing to enable other usages (including the dominant usage) by select actors.

What do these restrictionary hydrant designs look like? Basic fire hydrant usage involves first removing the outlet cap. To turn on the water flow, you must twist the "operating nut," usually set atop the hydrant, and usually requiring a large pentagonal wrench or a wrench that is otherwise unusual. (It is also often still possible to twist the operating nut, albeit more clumsily, with a big adjustable wrench.) Many redesign strategies involve locking off either the operating nut or the outlet cap, usually with a device

2. New York City Department of Environmental Protection 2011.

that requires a special key or wrench to disengage. For example, one restrictionary design strategy is to fit the hydrant with a specialized outlet cap that can only be easily removed with a specific and exclusively available wrench, such as a smooth, dome-shaped cap with no place to get a grip, save for special grooves designed for a particular tool. (This also functions to discourage cap theft.)

But perhaps the central design strategy for restricting hydrant usage is to cover up and lock the operating nut. This can be accomplished, for example, with specially designed covers that fit over the nut and are bolted closed with a padlock. (But fire departments sometimes complain that unlocking such mechanisms wastes valuable time.) A simpler mechanism is a metal cup built around the operating nut, thus requiring a special extended wrench that can reach down into the cup, preventing access with a standard adjustable wrench. A popular option is the Custodian Hydrant Lock, developed by a company called Hydra-Shield. It is a cover that fits over the operating nut and is mounted with a large nut of its own. This large secondary nut rotates freely by hand, independent of the operating nut. But with a special wrench, built with magnets inside, the Custodian can be twisted to engage the operating nut.

If these various hydrant locks can be conceived as restrictionary design modifications that close off certain stabilities, then it is also possible to identify unrestrictionary strategies that are taken up by competing social groups. Unauthorized users who are nevertheless determined to open a hydrant can find ways to circumvent the locks. Even in the case of the Custodian devices, with their thick metal covers and sophisticated magnet locking system, people have of course found ways to hack in with their own magnets and have developed bootleg tools for this purpose.[3]

But with all these dynamics in mind, it is crucial also to consider another approach to the issue of hydrants altogether. In New York

3. Fernandez 2010.

City, you can go to the local fire department and borrow a "spray cap" to install on your neighborhood hydrant. Or you can even request the fire department to come install one for you. (In some cases, it seems the fire department's assistance would be required, such as if your hydrant is fit with a lock, as many are in New York City.) The spray cap transforms the hydrant into a community sprinkler. The volume of water sprayed is of course greatly reduced, only one-fortieth the flow of an uncapped hydrant. And not only are spray caps legal but their use is seemingly encouraged.

And yet not everyone agrees with the wisdom of the spray cap program. For example, during heat waves, the city of Chicago would see thousands of unauthorized hydrant openings. That number dropped to the hundreds after Custodian locks were installed in the 1990s. The stated reasoning that city officials have provided for opposing a spray cap program is that it could have the side effect of encouraging illegal openings.[4] Chicago thus makes its priorities clear: discouraging unauthorized usage is more important than heat wave relief. And it has built these priorities into its infrastructure.

I suggest that the spray cap is neither a restrictionary nor an unrestrictionary modification but an exemplar of a third category. Where the hydrant locks close off a stability, and the hacks reopen that stability, the spray cap "opens up" the alternative stability, securing multiple usages. Let's refer to this kind of modification as an "expansionary" design modification.

Returning to the issue of homelessness, we can also find possibilities for expansionary strategies in public-space design. Think again of the design of garbage cans. We've seen examples of restrictionary design features, such as "rain hoods" and locking mechanisms that close off the cans from trash pickers. If a garbage can without a lock or lid maintains an alternative stability whereby it affords itself as a source for recyclable bottles or food scraps, then the restrictionary

---

4. Washburn 2004; Garcia 2007.

Figure 10. Garbage can with built-in external rack for recyclables in Copenhagen, Denmark. Photograph by the author.

modifications of the locks and rain hoods close off that stability. But some designers are working to do just the opposite.

Some garbage cans are designed with a separate and easily accessible rack or compartment for bottles and cans. Sometimes the design makes this function clear, and sometimes it is less noticeable. One example is a public garbage can whose exterior casing features a built-in external deposit rack. In Copenhagen, Denmark, external "deposit shelves" are being added to cans across the city. According to proponents, they allow easy and "dignified" access to recyclables.

After a trial run in 2015 that involved only a small handful of cans, the program has been deemed a success, garnering the support of 95 percent of Copenhageners and setting in motion plans for the installation of five hundred new racks.[5] Evidence that such designs can function on a large scale can be seen in San Francisco, where downtown areas feature garbage cans with separated and accessible compartments for recyclables. And the city does not collect the recyclable materials from those compartments; the contents are collected exclusively on a volunteer basis by people living unhoused.[6]

Of course, such policies and designs that encourage people to pick recycling from cans are noninnocent moves. For example, cities generate revenue through recycling, and the work of emptying cans throughout the city is someone's job. Offering that work and revenue to others is not without trade-offs, so as always, we must consider our values carefully and weigh out the possible consequences of our policy and design choices. In this case, it is important to keep in mind that recyclable materials from public cans represent a miniscule portion of a city's overall recycling efforts.

The example of the pro-pick garbage can designs shows that there are alternatives to the trend of antipick can design in particular, and to antihomeless design and policy in general. Some of the protest art projects reviewed herein point this way as well. It is possible to develop an expansionary pro-homeless approach toward public-space technologies and policies. What we need to do is step back and consider the values that should guide our design processes.

5. *Local* 2015.
6. Kane 2013.

7. Commendable Closure

IT COULD BE POSSIBLE at this point to gather an impression that expansionary designs are somehow always preferable to restrictionary ones. This is not the case. Spelling out *why* will help to clarify what it means for values to guide our design and policy development practices, all while keeping in mind the multistability of technology.

Let's consider the design of fences that stand along the sides of bridges and, in particular, the fact that such fences often arc inward. This inward curve can serve several purposes. For one, it can discourage people from throwing things off the bridge, which can of course be extremely dangerous. If someone were to throw, say, an object off an overpass, it could land on passing cars below and cause an accident.

But there is a further reason to arc bridge fences inward: to discourage people themselves from climbing up and over. The act of jumping off a bridge is of course a common form of suicide. Bridge fences and other redesigns, referred to as "suicide barriers," have proven to be an effective deterrent.

There is a long-standing and intense debate over the prospect of building a suicide barrier along the Golden Gate Bridge in San Francisco, California. Since the bridge first opened in the 1930s, an estimated sixteen hundred people have jumped to their deaths, second in the world only to the Nanjing Yangtze River Bridge in China. Proponents for a barrier have been arguing their case for decades.

Opponents of suicide barriers on bridges in general, and on the Golden Gate Bridge in particular, tend to offer two main arguments. First, they claim that the barriers will detract from the beauty of a manmade landmark. And second, they claim that those seeking suicide will simply find another location; that is, they suggest that the measure will not actually have an effect on individuals contemplating suicide nor an effect on regional suicide rates.

On the first point, we can only attempt to weigh the value of public health against the value of architecture aesthetics. But on the second point, we can turn to data. Jane Pirkis and her colleagues have conducted a meta-analysis of studies investigating the effectiveness of suicide barriers on regional rates and conclude that, "although there may be some shifting of suicidal acts to other sites, deaths by the same method are still significantly reduced overall."[1] This accords with the psychological realities of suicide prevention.[2] Efforts to intervene on suicide attempts, and efforts to make options for suicide less easily available, reduce overall rates.

This point is illustrated dramatically by the oft discussed moment in British history when coal ovens were phased out in favor of natural gas in the 1960s. Before this shift, a common means of suicide was asphyxiation through oven gas. The high carbon monoxide level in coal gas made it a method readily available in many homes. So when the country shifted from coal gas to natural gas, a substance without the same carbon monoxide content, there was a massive drop in overall suicides. While it is true that the rate of suicide by

1. Pirkis et al. 2015, 999.
2. In a 2013 meta-analysis, Georgina R. Cox and her colleagues summarize their findings as follows: "The strongest evidence for effectiveness comes from studies that have looked at restricting access to means through the installation of barriers at jumping sites and on railway networks. This body of evidence consistently suggests that these measures are associated with a reduction in suicides at these sites because they limit access or make it difficult to perform suicidal acts. In the main, the evidence also suggests that restricting access to means at one site does not drive suicidal individuals to seek alternative locations, thereby shifting the problem elsewhere. There are also indications that reducing suicides by a particular method does not lead to substitution of different methods; instead it may have a positive impact on the overall suicide rate" (10).

other means did increase during this time, the increase not nearly enough to compensate for the absence of oven-related deaths. The overall rate across the United Kingdom dropped by one-third and has remained that way.[3] We can see something similar in data on the Golden Gate Bridge in particular; a study of potential jumpers pulled or talked down from the bridge by police found more than 90 percent to have ultimately continued their lives.[4]

In 2014, officials approved a plan to construct a barrier system on the Golden Gate Bridge that will include nets that stretch twenty feet out on both sides. Set to a price of $76 million, the project currently remains encumbered with delays.[5]

Bridge fences are another example of a restrictionary public-space design. In one case, it is a design modification of the bridge to restrict those who may want to toss an object over the side and endanger the people below. In the second case, fences and other redesign features function as suicide barriers, closing off the bridge as a method for self-harm. In both cases (and in others we can go back and pick out of previous chapters, such as the antiterrorism garbage can designs), we find restrictionary modifications intended to close off options for harming oneself or others. In both cases we may find the protection from harm to be commendable.

In these bridge fence examples, the restrictionary designs can be interpreted as a majority population (e.g., those driving or walking below) protecting themselves from a minority population (those who want to do harm to strangers by throwing things off bridges) or as a majority population (the state) protecting a minority population (those who would commit suicide by jumping from a bridge) from themselves. But of course, this is not the only possible directionality of power for commendable restrictionary designs; restrictionary designs can also close off stabilities preferred by a powerful majority.

3. Anderson 2008; Kreitman 1976.
4. Seiden 1978.
5. Cabanatuan 2014.

Consider the example of bicycle lane development in the United States. In 2013, more than seven hundred people were killed in traffic accidents while riding a bicycle, and forty thousand were injured.[6] One way to help protect riders, to encourage ridership, and thus also to promote a more environmentally friendly form of transportation is to expand the country's networks of bike lanes. But as we've seen with any public-space design, bike lanes will be open to different meanings and uses. It can be helpful to think of the bike lane as a multistable technology.[7]

A bike lane is a space of the road designated for bike riders, and there is debate about which lane designs are best, whether there should be barriers, and so on. Let's here consider a standard bike lane, set along the side of the roadway and divided only by a painted line. And let's take biking on the bike lane to be the dominant stability. Under this conception, there is an alternative stability frequently taken up in practice: bike lanes are often used as makeshift parking spots for cars. In the American context, in which cyclists are still a small minority, and for which the political struggle to establish bike lanes remains a challenge, it can be disheartening to find bike lanes coopted as parking spots. As Rebecca Serna, executive director of the Atlanta Bicycle Coalition, puts it, "bike lanes, like sidewalks, set aside space to make it safer and easier to bike places. Every time someone parks in a bike lane (or on a sidewalk!), it threatens that progress."[8]

What makes this an enlightening example at this juncture of the pamphlet is that what I've labeled the "dominant" stability—biking in the bike lane—is not the usage taken up by the most powerful group of travelers (drivers) but the one used by a transportation minority (cyclists). In the American context, the bike lane

6. Goodwin et al. 2015.

7. This point is inspired by the work of cycling advocate and policy researcher Caroline Appleton, from whom I have learned everything I know about bike lane policy.

8. Serna 2014.

is a device designed for and utilized by a marginalized group, at least compared to the supremacy of car culture and infrastructure. When cars park in bike lanes, it is an example of a more powerful group taking up an alternative stability.

There are bike lane designs that, in addition to making lanes safer, also discourage or even prevent their use as a parking spot. For example, there are "protected" lanes, enclosed by concrete barriers. Sometimes bollards or other standing posts mark off a bike lane. These can be understood as restrictionary designs that simultaneously allow the lane to be used for biking but discourage or prevent a car from entering. And as always, there are trade-offs to consider, such as the fact that a concrete bike lane barrier would prevent all cars, including emergency vehicles, from using the lane as a parking spot. There are compromise designs available too, such as a series of bumps or a slightly raised lane, which would discourage a bike lane's use as a parking spot (though not physically prevent it, as would a concrete barrier) and would simultaneously allow usage by emergency vehicles.

The example of bike lane barriers shows that it is possible in some cases for restrictionary designs to protect a minority of users against a more powerful majority. Put differently, restrictionary designs do not always work to preserve hierarchies; in some cases, they have the potential to challenge them. In the previous section, we saw examples of expansionary designs that can, at least in certain ways, be interpreted to challenge rather than preserve existing hierarchies. Whereas antipick garbage cans and hydrant locks close off stabilities favored by less powerful groups, the pro-pick cans and spray caps were offered as examples of expansionary designs that facilitate usage in just those terms, in addition to retaining the dominant usage. In contrast, an expansionary approach to bike lane design might encourage exploitation of these spaces by drivers, the already advantaged group. Restrictionary bike lane barriers may thus in this case actually challenge the existing hierarchy by closing off a stability that represents an encroachment by the more powerful network.

The point here is that restrictionary, unrestrictionary, expansionary, and any other forms of technological modification do not automatically instantiate particular values. It will depend on the case and on our perspective on that case.

8. Values

DESIGNS AND REGULATIONS are used to influence behavior all the time and all across the various contexts of our world. Supermarkets and casinos routinely lack windows and clocks to encourage you to lose track of time and stay longer. Movies include musical scores that enhance the emotion of the drama on-screen. Airports and other highly trafficked buildings often include subtle clues to keep people moving along through them in the right direction.

These kinds of manipulations are everywhere. Some are easy to notice. Others are easy to miss. Some are harmless or even helpful. Others are harmful and should be opposed. In this pamphlet, I have tried to develop some conceptual tools for identifying a particular kind of material situation: technologies that are open to multiple uses, and the social and political forces that influence the availability of those potential uses. And I have tried to outline a particular understanding of technological "guilt," one that considers a technology's various possible purposes and that also considers the device's relationships to particular collective agendas and larger political structures, agendas and structures open to charges of callousness and cruelty. I hope that these ideas can be of assistance in evaluating concrete technologies and technological trends. In addition to public-space design, there is potential application to a variety of other contexts, including workplaces, classrooms, prisons, the home, and the online environment. And these ideas could be usefully connected to the emerging literature on design practices that maintain sensitivity to values and that work to include others in the design process.[1]

1. For examples of work on value-sensitive design, see Brey 2009;

Through this perspective, I have attempted to put a spotlight on a particular political strategy: antihomeless design.

The argument of this pamphlet has been a negative one; it is a criticism of what I claim to be a large-scale pattern of design and law in cities across the world. I have attempted to identify and philosophically articulate a pervasive strategy in which antihomeless design and policy effectively push unhoused people out of public spaces, often performed in such a way that it can be difficult to notice if you are not among the targeted minority. And I have attempted to reveal this strategy to be immoral and unjust.

Obviously, this is only a small part of the larger story of the problem of homelessness. I do not mean to imply that antihomeless design and law are somehow the only—or even the most major—*cause* of homelessness. Nor should it be implied that the removal of antihomeless designs would by itself somehow be a solution to the problem. Nor are unhoused people themselves the only victims of this problem, as, for example, small businesses and churches struggle to cope with this failure on the part of our national and city governments, large corporations, and other societal institutions.

But I do hope that by calling attention to the often unnoticed elements of antihomeless design and law in our cities, two things might be accomplished.

One, by exposing these often unnoticed designs and laws, and by highlighting their pervasiveness and the concerted way they work together to target the unhoused population, I hope to issue a test of our ethical intuitions. Insofar as we are appalled by any parts of these treatments of human beings, we should connect

---

JafariNaimi, Nathan, and Hargraves 2015; Wittkower 2016; Simon 2017. In addition to "values," we could also approach this "technomoral" situation, as Shannon Vallor calls it, through the development of "virtuous" character. See Vallor 2016. Because public space itself can be seen as a rapidly shifting context of technology and policy, the best stable guide for action may be the cultivation of a moral sense of what kind of people we want to be.

that reaction with the knowledge that those treatments are part of a systematic strategy used—to different degrees and in different ways—by cities all over the world. The injustice and immorality of these strategies for addressing the problem of homelessness are made clear. And although the work of opposing these strategies is only one small piece of a better solution, it is an opposition we should nonetheless take up.

Two, the analysis of this particular aspect of the problem has the potential to help clarify and crystalize the values that should guide our approach to larger solutions. Let's conclude with an enumeration of a few of the policies and approaches that appear consistent with the values that have emerged through the course of this pamphlet.

The values emerging herein call for us to expect and to oppose new efforts to target the unhoused. We should resist utopian thinking in general, and progress narratives about the problem of homelessness in particular, and keep watch for new efforts to roll back assistance programs for the unhoused.

At the time of this writing, the Trump administration has recently assumed power in the United States. In light of the values emerging herein, this is cause for concern; the Trump campaign's rhetoric and the administration's early actions have targeted minorities, women, and immigrants. The Trump administration's attorney general, who serves as the head the DOJ, has a documented history of opposition to civil rights legislation and criminal justice reform. The secretary of housing and urban development is as qualified for the job as me or you. (Or less so, if you happen to have any qualifications whatsoever.) Thus, at the national level, there is reason to remain watchful for new efforts to target the homeless and reason not to assume that new protections are on the way. And there is all the more reason to push for reform at the local level, because new national-level protections may now be even less likely.[2]

2. Rosenberger 2017b; Serwer 2017; Kilgore 2017; Bouie 2017.

The values exposed in this pamphlet should additionally lead us to strongly support "Right to Rest" initiatives.[3] This refers to efforts to legislate our commitment against antihomeless laws that criminalize basic behaviors of the unhoused. Right to Rest legislation, or a "Homeless Bill of Rights," as it is also sometimes called, could effectively overturn and outlaw antihomeless policies, such as camping bans and sit/lie laws. Resistance to the increasing criminalization of homelessness is an important priority.

The values that emerge from the analysis in this pamphlet also appear consistent with a "housing-first" approach to the problem of homelessness.[4] This tactic involves getting unhoused people into housing as the initial step, in contrast to traditional programs that attempt to shepherd people out of homelessness in stages, through the shelter system and transitional housing, with each step subject to scrutiny. For example, traditional approaches can include requiring people to defeat addiction, or complete multistep programs, before becoming eligible for more permanent housing. The housing-first model turns this logic upside down. The understanding is that if an unhoused person can get into housing, then other conditions can be better treated. That is, though many problems may keep a person unhoused, the act of providing housing to this person can be the strongest first part of a solution to those problems. And, perhaps counterintuitively, a housing-first approach appears to be the cheaper option. When the costs of sheltering, law enforcement, criminal prosecution, and repeated emergency medical services are added together, the expense of simply providing unhoused people with housing

3. At the time of this writing, three states in the United States maintain a Homeless Bill of Rights: Connecticut, Rhode Island, and Illinois. https://www.cga.ct.gov/2013/TOB/S/2013SB-00896-R00-SB.htm; http://webserver.rilin.state.ri.us/Statutes/TITLE34/34-37.1/INDEX.HTM; http://www.ilga.gov/legislation/ilcs/ilcs3.asp?ActID=3517&ChapterID=64.

4. For a helpful primer on housing-first initiatives, see Carrier 2015. For the U.S. federal government's adoption of this perspective, see https://www.usich.gov/tools-for-action/opening-doors.

is cost-effective. This is what was found in Utah's pioneering housing-first program, an effort that has become the poster child for this perspective, reporting a 91 percent drop in chronic homelessness since 2005.[5]

At the same time, housing-first programs may not be a panacea. The unhoused population is diverse, with people in a multitude of completely different situations. The values exposed in this pamphlet thus additionally seem consistent with the support of shelters and other more traditional outreach efforts, because these offer real and crucial assistance to many people.[6] But we should also remain critical of shelter policies, because they have significant effects on the lives of their clients and contribute to determining who can and cannot use these facilities. And as we have seen, the policies of local shelters (and their particular capacity limits) affect the legal status of the unhoused people who cannot or do not use them. Another demand that appears consistent with the preceding values is the recognition that those living outside areas with high unhoused populations (e.g., urban centers, neighborhoods with shelters) should share responsibility for addressing the problem of homelessness, including the financial responsibility.

With a problem as complex and fraught as homelessness, it should come as no surprise to see that any solutions on offer are only partial, ongoing, and imperfect. To move forward, it is important to spell out our values and keep hold of them as we as a community address the problem. And we must keep hold of them as well as we learn to see the strategies of law and design already in place all around us that conflict with those values.

5. Glionna 2015.
6. Smith 2016.

Bibliography

Akrich, Madeleine. 1992. "The De-Scription of Technical Artifacts." In *Shaping Technology/Building Society*, edited by Wiebe E. Bijker and John Law, pp. 205–24. Cambridge, Mass.: MIT Press.

Alcoff, Linda Martín. 2006. *Visible Identities: Race, Gender, and the Self.* Oxford: Oxford University Press.

Anderson, Scott. 2008. "The Urge to End It All." *New York Times Magazine*, July 6, MM38. http://www.nytimes.com/2008/07/06/magazine/06suicide-t.html.

Bordo, Susan. 1997. *Twilight Zones: The Hidden Life of Cultural Images from Plato to O.J.* Berkeley: University of California Press.

Borgmann, Albert. 2007. "Interview with Albert Borgmann." In *Philosophy of Technology: 5 Questions*, edited by Jan Kyrre Berg Olsen and Evan Selinger, 7–15. New York: Automatic Press/VIP.

Bouie, Jamelle. 2017. "Ben Carson Knows Nothing." *Slate*, January 12. http://www.slate.com/articles/news_and_politics/politics/2017/01/ben_carson_future_hud_secretary_knows_nothing_about_hud.html.

Brey, Philip. 2009. "Values in Technology and Disclosive Computer Ethics." In *Cambridge Handbook of Information and Computer Ethics*, edited by L. Floridi, 41–58. Cambridge: Cambridge University Press.

Cabanatuan, Michael. 2014. "Golden Gate Bridge Board OKs $76 Million for Suicide Barrier." *San Francisco Chronicle*, June 28. http://www.sfgate.com/bayarea/article/Golden-Gate-Bridge-going-to-get-suicide-nets-5585482.php.

Carlson, Jen. 2015. "Photos: Sharp Anti-Homeless Spikes Have Been Installed Near Pope's Route." *Gothamist*, September 25. http://gothamist.com/2015/09/25/pope_spikes_hobo_b_gone.php.

Carrier, Scott. 2015. "Room for Improvement." *Mother Jones*, March/April. http://www.motherjones.com/politics/2015/02/housing-first-solution-to-homelessness-utah.

Casper, Monica J., and Lisa Jean Moore. 2009. *Missing Bodies: The Politics of Visibility*. New York: New York University Press.

Chellew, Cara. 2016. "Design Paranoia." *Ontario Planning Journal* 31, no. 5: 18–20.

Collins, Patricia Hill. 1986. "Learning for the Outsider Within: The Sociological Significance of Black Feminist Thought." *Social Problems* 33, no. 6: S14–S32.

Cox, Georgina R., Christabel Owens, Jo Robinson, Angela Nicholas, Anne Lockley, Michelle Williamson, Yee Tak Derek Cheung, and Jane Pirkis. 2013. "Interventions to Reduce Suicides at Suicide Hotspots: A Systematic Review." *BMC Public Health* 13, Article 214. http://bmcpublichealth.biomedcentral.com/articles/10.1186/1471-2458-13-214.

Davis, Mike. 1990. *City of Quartz: Excavating the Future in Los Angeles*. London: Verso.

DiSalvo, Carl. 2012. *Adversarial Design*. Cambridge, Mass.: MIT Press.

Duneier, Mitchell. 1999. *Sidewalk*. New York: Farrar, Straus, and Giroux.

Durso, Laura E., and Gary J. Gates. 2012. *Serving Our Youth: Findings from a National Survey of Service Providers Working with Lesbian, Gay, Bisexual, and Transgender Youth Who Are Homeless or at Risk of Becoming Homeless*. Los Angeles: Williams Institute with True Colors Fund and Palette Fund. http://williamsinstitute.law.ucla.edu/wp-content/uploads/Durso-Gates-LGBT-Homeless-Youth-Survey-July-2012.pdf.

Fagen, Kevin. 2015. "Dousing Homeless at Church Gets S.F. Archdiocese in Hot Water." *San Francisco Chronicle*, March 18. http://www.sfgate.com/bayarea/article/S-F-archdiocese-will-stop-dousing-homeless-6143213.php.

Feenberg, Andrew. 1999. *Questioning Technology*. New York: Routledge.

Fernandez, Manny. 2010. "Cracking the Locks on Relief." *New York Times*, September 6, MB1. http://www.nytimes.com/2010/08/08/nyregion/08ritual.html.

Foscarinis, Maria. 2015. *In Just Times*, November. http://www.nlchp.org/IJT/2015November.

Garcia, Monique. 2007. "City Tries to Douse a Summer Tradition." *Chicago Tribune*, July 22. http://articles.chicagotribune.com/2007-07-22/news/0707210403_1_open-hydrants-water-park-neighborhoods.

Glionna, John M. 2015. "Utah Is Winning the War on Chronic Homelessness with 'Housing First' Program." *LA Times*, May 24. http://www.latimes.com/nation/la-na-utah-housing-first-20150524-story.html.

Goldensohn, Rosa. 2013. "Strand Books Used Sprinklers to Douse the Homeless, Employees Say." *DNAinfo* (blog), November 14. https://www.dnainfo.com/new-york/20131114/greenwich-village/strand-books-yanks-warning-signs-for-sprinklers-used-douse-homeless.

Goodwin, Arthur, Libby Thomas, Bevan Kirley, William Hall, Natalie O'Brien, and Katie Hill. 2015. *Countermeasures That Work: A Highway Safety Countermeasure Guide for State Highway Safety Offices.* 8th ed. Report DOT HS 812 202. Washington, D.C.: National Highway Traffic Safety Administration.

Greater Vancouver Transportation Authority. 2007. "Universally Accessible Bus Stop Design Guidelines." Project Report, Final Draft. http://www.translink.ca/~/media/Documents/rider_guide/access_transit/Universally%20Accessible%20Bus%20Stop%20Design%20Guidelines.ashx.

Halliday, Josh, and Haroon Siddique. 2014. "Boris Johnson Calls for Removal of Anti-Homeless Spikes." *The Guardian,* June 9. http://www.theguardian.com/society/2014/jun/09/boris-johnson-calls-removal-anti-homeless-spikes.

Haraway, Donna, ed. 2004. "The Promises of Monsters: A Regenerative Politics for Inappropriate/D Others." In *The Haraway Reader,* 63–124. New York: Routledge.

Harding, Sandra. 1995. "'Strong Objectivity': A Response to the New Objectivity Question." *Synthese* 104, no. 3: 331–49.

Hasse, Cathrine. 2015. *An Anthropology of Learning: On Nested Frictions in Cultural Ecologies.* Dordrecht, Netherlands: Springer.

Hayakawa, Yumiko. 2006. "Public Benches Turn 'Anti-Homeless.'" *OhMyNews,* October 15. http://english.ohmynews.com/articleview/article_view.asp.

Heidegger, Martin. 2000. *Being and Time.* Translated by John Macquarre and Edward Robinson. Oxford: Blackwell.

Ihde, Don. 1990. *Technology and the Lifeworld.* Bloomington: Indiana University Press.

———. 1999. "Technology and Prognostic Predicaments." *AI & Society,* 13: 44–51.

———. 2009. *Postphenomenology and Technoscience: The Peking University Lectures.* New York: State University of New York Press.

JafariNaimi, Nassim, Lisa Nathan, and Ian Hargraves. 2015. "Values as Hypotheses: Design, Inquiry, and the Service of Values." *Design Issues* 31, no. 4: 91–104.

Kane, Will. 2013. "SF Doesn't Recycle Trash in Public Cans." *San Francisco Chronicle,* April 3. http://www.sfgate.com/bayarea/article/SF-doesn-t-recycle-trash-in-public-cans-4407747.php.

Kilgore, Ed. 2017. "Sessions as Attorney General Means Criminal-Justice Reform Is Dead." *New York Magazine,* November 18. http://nymag.com/daily/intelligencer/2016/11/sessions-as-ag-means-criminal-justice-reform-is-dead.html.

Kreitman, Norma. 1976. "The Coal Gas Story: United Kingdom Suicide Rates, 1960–1971." *British Journal of Preventative and Social Medicine* 30: 86–93.

Lambert, Léopold. 2013. *Cruel Designs*. The Funambulist Pamphlets 7. New York: Punctum Books.

Latour, Bruno. 1992. "Where Are the Missing Masses? The Sociology of a Few Mundane Artifacts." In *Shaping Technology/Building Society*, edited by Wiebe Bijker and John Law, 226–58. London: MIT Press.

Lazo, Luz. 2013. "Push for Sidewalks in Hyattsville Faces Resistance in One Neighborhood." *Washington Post*, April 15. https://www .washingtonpost.com/local/push-for-sidewalks-in-hyattsville-faces -resistance-in-one-neighborhood/2013/04/15/fec937b8-9d57-11e2 -9a79-eb5280c81c63_story.html.

Local. 2015. "Copenhagen's 'Dignified' Rubbish Plan Expands." October 26. http://www.thelocal.dk/20151026/copenhagens-dignified-rubbish -plan-expands.

Merleau-Ponty, Maurice. 1945. *The Phenomenology of Perception*. Translated by D. Landes. London: Routledge.

National Law Center on Homelessness and Poverty. 2014. *No Safe Place: The Criminalization of Homelessness in the United States*. http://www .nlchp.org/documents/No_Safe_Place.

New York City Department of Environmental Protection. 2011. "DEP Kicks Off 2011 Summer Fire Hydrant Abuse Campaign." Press Release 11-59. July 14. http://www.nyc.gov/html/dep/html/press_releases/11 -59pr.shtml.

Oudshoorn, Nelly, and Trevor Pinch. 2003. "Introduction: How Users and Non-Users Matter." In *How Users Matter: The Co-Construction of Users and Technology*, edited by Nelly Oudshoorn and Trevor Pinch, 1–28. Cambridge, Mass.: MIT Press.

Petty, James. 2016. "The London Spikes Controversy: Homelessness, Urban Securitization and the Question of 'Hostile Architecture.'" *International Journal for Crime, Justice and Social Democracy* 5, no. 1: 67–81.

Pirkis, Jane, Lay San Too, Matthew J. Spittal, Karolina Krysinska, Jo Robinson, and Yee Tak Derek Cheung. 2015. "Interventions to Reduce Suicides at Suicide Hotspots: A Systematic Review and Meta-Analysis." *The Lancet Psychiatry* 2, no. 11: 994–1001.

QMI Agency. 2014. "Montreal Removes Anti-homeless Spikes from Downtown Bookstore." *Toronto Sun*, June 10. http://www.torontosun. com/2014/06/10/montreal-removes-anti-homeless-spikes-from- downtown-bookstore.

Quinn, Ben. 2014. "Anti-Homeless Spikes Are Part of a Wider Phenomenon of 'Hostile Architecture.'" *The Guardian*, June 13. https://www .theguardian.com/artanddesign/2014/jun/13/anti-homeless-spikes -hostile-architecture.

Reinan, John. 2014. "Fight over Suburban Sidewalks a Window in 21st Century Life." *Seattle Times*, November 28. http://www.seattletimes

.com/nation-world/fight-over-suburban-sidewalks-a-window-onto
-21st-century-life/.

Riverside Transit Agency. 2015. "Bus Stop Design Guidelines." August.
http://www.riversidetransit.com/images/stories/DOWNLOADS
/PUBLICATIONS/DESIGN_GUIDES/Design%20Guidelines%20-%20
Aug%202015.pdf.

Rosenberger, Robert. 2014a. "How Cities Use Design to Drive Homeless
People Away." *The Atlantic,* June 19. http://www.theatlantic.com
/business/archive/2014/06/how-cities-use-design-to-drive-homeless
-people-away/373067/.

———. 2014b. "Multistability and the Agency of Mundane Artifacts: From
Speed Bumps to Subway Benches." *Human Studies* 37: 369–92.

———. 2015. "No Camping and Other Laws that Sneakily Push Away the
Homeless." *The Atlantic,* September 25. http://www.theatlantic.com
/business/archive/2015/10/no-camping-and-other-laws-that-sneakily
-push-the-homeless-away/412216/.

———. 2017a. "On the Hermeneutics of Everyday Things: or, The
Philosophy of Fire Hydrants." *AI & Society* 32: 233–41.

———. 2017b. "Review of *The Bill of Rights: The Fight to Secure America's
Liberties* by Carol Berkin." *The Rumpus,* January 19. http://therumpus
.net/2017/01/the-bill-of-rights-the-fight-to-secure-americas-liberties
-by-carol-berkin/.

Rosenberger, Robert, and Peter-Paul Verbeek, eds. 2015.
*Postphenomenological Investigations: Essays on Human-Technology
Relations.* Lanham, Md.: Lexington Books/Rowman Littlefield.

Savicic, Gordan, and Selena Savic, eds. 2013. *Unpleasant Design.* Belgrade:
GLORIA.

Seiden, Richard H. 1978. "Where Are They Now? A Follow-Up Study of
Suicide Attempters from the Golden Gate Bridge." *Suicide and Life
Threatening Behavior* 8, no. 4: 203–16.

Serna, Rebecca. 2014. "Stop Parking in Bike Lanes, Atlanta." *Creative
Loafing: Atlanta* (blog), October 30. http://clatl.com/atlanta/stop
-parking-in-bike-lanes-atlanta/Content?oid=12609779.

Serwer, Adam. 2017. "The Cynical Selling of Jeff Sessions as a Civil-Rights
Champion." *The Atlantic,* February 10. https://www.theatlantic.com
/politics/archive/2017/02/the-fiction-of-jeff-sessions-civil-rights
-champion/516237/.

Sewell, Cynthia. 2015. "Judge Dismisses Lawsuit against Boise Ordinance
Prohibiting Camping in Public Places." *Idaho Statesman,* September 30.
http://www.idahostatesman.com/news/local/article41571171.html.

Simon, Judith. 2017. "Value-Sensitive Design and Responsible
Research and Innovation." In *The Ethics of Technology: Methods and
Approaches,* edited by S. O. Hansson, 219–35. London: Roman and
Littlefield.

Smith, Doug. 2016. "Is the Shift to Permanent Housing Making L.A.'s
    Homelessness Problem Even Worse?" *LA Times*, August 15. http://
    www.latimes.com/local/lanow/la-me-ln-transitional-housing
    -cutbacks-20160815-snap-story.html.

Star, Susan Leigh. 1990. "Power, Technology and the Phenomenology of
    Conventions: On Being Allergic to Onions." *Sociological Review* 38, no.
    S1: 26–56.

Vallor, Shannon. 2016. *Technology and the Virtues*. Oxford: Oxford
    University Press.

Verbeek, Peter-Paul. 2011. *Moralizing Technology: Understanding and
    Designing the Morality of Things*. Chicago: Chicago University Press.

Washburn, Gary. 2004. "City's Hydrants Getting a New Lock." *Chicago
    Tribune*, November 6. http://articles.chicagotribune.com/2004-11-26
    /news/0411260108_1_open-hydrants-locking-devices.

Whyte, Kyle Powys. 2015. "What Is Multistability? A Theory of
    the Keystone Concept of Postphenomenological Research." In
    Technoscience and Postphenomenology: The Manhattan Papers, edited
    by Jan Kyrre Berg Olsen Friis and Robert P. Crease, 69–81. New York:
    Lexington Books.

Winner, Langdon. 1993. "Upon Opening the Black Box and Finding It
    Empty: Social Constructivism and the Philosophy of Technology."
    Science, Technology, and Human Values 18, no. 3: 362–78.

Winnipeg Transit. 2006. "Designing for Sustainable Transportation and
    Transit in Winnipeg." January. http://winnipegtransit.com/public
    _content/pdfs/WinnipegTransit_sustainabledesign.pdf.

Wittkower, Dylan E. 2016. "Principles of Anti-discriminatory Design."
    In *2016 IEEE International Symposium on Ethics in Engineering,
    Science, and Technology*. Piscataway, N.J.: IEEE. doi:10.1109/
    ETHICS.2016.7560055.

Wright, Samantha, and Associated Press. 2015. "City Weighs in on DOJ
    Criticism of Boise Homeless Camping Law." Boise State Public Radio,
    August 7. http://boisestatepublicradio.org/post/city-weighs-doj
    -criticism-boise-homeless-camping-law.

Acknowledgments

For essential comments and conversations about this work, I extend special thanks to Don Ihde, Sabrina Hom, Chad Kautzer, Caroline Appleton, Jesper Aagaard, Mario Bianchini, and Sylvia and Thomas Hom. Thanks must also go to the folks from the postphenomenology research group and many others for sending ideas and pictures from around the planet. I deeply appreciate the work of the people at the University of Minnesota Press on this book and for guidance from my editors Danielle Kasprzak at Minnesota and Rebecca Rosen at *The Atlantic*. My appreciation as well goes to artists Sarah Ross and Fabian Brunsing for permission to use their images. This project was helpfully nudged along by support from the Georgia Tech Center for Urban Innovation.

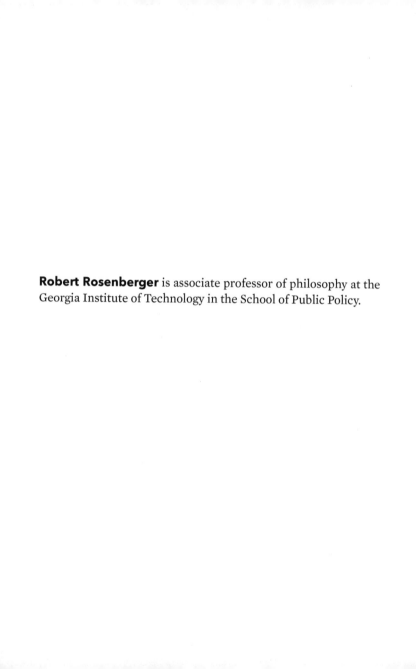

Robert Rosenberger is associate professor of philosophy at the Georgia Institute of Technology in the School of Public Policy.